THE ME IN MOTHERHOOD

FLOW BELINSKY

THE ME IN MOTHERHOOD

A MEMOIR

atmosphere press

Thank you to my husband and my daughter for helping me become the woman I am.

part 1

SEARCHING

august 2019

Where is the Me in Motherhood?

It may be there,
if you squint hard enough
or delete a bunch of letters,
string together distant parts.

It might be there,
if you carve in like an old oak
or twist the gnarly branches,
revealing a different shape.

It could be there,
if you changed the ancient meaning,
walked boldly into the future,
and healed the lineage of our time.

It can be there,
if you scratch away expectations,
shake up the established order,
and make a new way to live.

It will be seen,
if you plant something else there
in the middle, in the beginning,
or in your very own mind.

It's surely there,
if you dream new definitions,
invent a different language,
if you write it with your life.

rebel

I am sitting surrounded by filth. There are stains on the placemats. Dust on the table. Crumbs and chunks of crackers under my slippered feet. I don't care.

I am typing. I am writing something. I am letting my fingers move gracefully, a clicking rhythm section in the orchestra of my creativity. At this point, it doesn't matter what comes out, as long as my hands are moving, as long as my mind is grooving with the music of the making rather than getting caught in a rut again.

Most days I wake up and clean. This place is never clean. There is always something to clean.

I wake up and put the dishes away. I wipe the counters. I wash the pans. Something always has to be done. It's never done.

I wake up and immediately get to work. I barely stretch anymore. I barely notice the beauty out the window. I don't delight in a new day. I don't feel grateful to be alive. I just get up and clean and take care of people.

Today, I didn't. Today, I let the mess be. Today, my

husband took our kid out to breakfast and I stayed in bed an extra half hour. I got up and frowned. I scratched my head, then my pubes. I looked around for my robe, put it on. I stumbled out and saw the mess. I almost went right to it, but then I didn't. I didn't touch a thing. I made my coffee around the plates on the counter. I filled the kettle by reaching over the pot in the sink.

As my cup of joe brewed, I smiled. Not a big one, just a subtle turn of the lips from down to up. I felt a surge of power. I sauntered into the living room, kicked a stuffed animal out of the way, and danced. I hadn't danced in months.

I moved to no music, just a beat in my mind, swaying my hips, moving my arms wildly above my head. I twirled around, sashayed a bit, laughed at myself, stepped on a lego. Suddenly I felt a surge of anger. A surge of grief. A surge of hatred for the never-ending work of motherhood.

"Fuck it!" I declared to the empty house. "Fuck it all!" I threw my arms in the air.

Then I got out my computer, sat down with my coffee, and began to write.

truth

I am having a small nervous breakdown. It's not as big as the others. I'm not fully losing it this time—but almost. Sometimes it seeps out of my eyes in a frenzied mess of tears and complexity. Sometimes the fist in my belly clamps down so hard I moan in pain. Sometimes my breath is short and quick, my thoughts racing—desperate.

I need to get away from everyone and everything. I am annoyed by the smallest sounds. I am a mother, a caregiver, every day. Even though I have help, it's not enough. Even though I only have one kid, it's too much for me. I'm stressed out, worn out, beat up. I need a long vacation.

Right now, the song "Vacation" is playing on the radio in this coffee shop where I'm sitting.

"Vacation all I ever wanted, vacation have to get away." Yeah, that. That's what I want. Permanently.

Yet...not. I love my family. I like my life. I love being with them. But I also don't. I also hate it and want to go away forever. The dichotomy is tearing at me, eating my insides. I am holding so much tension that I can't even poop without coffee. I am grappling with too much duality of desire. I want my old life back, my own mind back. I want to be able to focus on myself, my work, my contribution to the world besides this endless cooking, cleaning, and childcare. But I also like being a mom; like focusing on other people; like taking care of them. I want to have both exclusively at the same time.

———

Nowadays, when I get time off, I don't know how to be alone. I'm too pent up, worked up—tight and wound. It's uncomfortable to relax. I always feel like I need to be doing something, cleaning something, helping someone, listening or paying attention to something else. When it's time to focus on myself, I can't. I'm too far gone, hidden behind all the tension, buried under all these feelings that I haven't had space to feel for days or weeks while I was tending to others. A vacation wouldn't be enough. I would come right back into this on the other side.

That's what happened when I went to a healing resort in Mexico with my husband last year. We were there for five whole days. We left our year-old daughter with my mother. They have bonded deeply since her birth. It was fine. I know, leaving her for a week when she is that young may seem strange. Most moms these days barely leave their kids for an hour, breastfeed forever, sleep together. I'm not like them.

It was huge for me to get away like that, so healing to my body, mind, and nervous system. I relaxed in ways I hadn't in over a year. The fresh mountain air, the big trees lining the clean brick paths, the beautiful flower arrangements—all brought peace. Chef-made meals garnished with tropical fruit delighted my taste buds; the lack of dish-doing softened my hands. The warmth of the hot tubs revived me. The care of masseuses melted my tight muscles. The quiet room with no children eased my frazzled nerves. I felt almost like myself again.

I cried the last day. I didn't want to come back, because I knew. I knew I would get all wound up again. But it was more than that. The community of the resort had healed me too. Seeing people on the trails, saying *hello*'s and *how are you*'s, getting to know them better over long dinners— all of it made me feel connected and taken care of, a part of something bigger than one single household.

We have been quite isolated since we became parents. Somehow, friendships and community fell away. They were still there, but not up close—distant, impersonal. We were left with just ourselves and occasionally our parents. Sometimes I basked in the quiet house while the baby napped and sometimes I cried from loneliness.

We were lucky to have our parents close by for our daughter's first year of life, but it's never been enough. We need more people. We need togetherness. We need singing and dancing and hugging and loving and helping each other—a sense of tribe. It's in our DNA. We all need that. Without it, parenting is torture. It's too much for me. It's too much for any of us.

We are moving soon, leaving San Diego and following my parents up to Bend, Oregon. They moved there five months ago and left us here in the sweltering heat with not enough child-care, not enough breaks.

My husband and I are Southern California natives. We each moved away for about ten years for college and adventures after. We moved back around the same time and met each other three years ago. We dated for less than a year, got pregnant, got married. Now we live north of San Diego, in a dry desert place full of small taupe buildings and faded signs, eucalyptus and succulents, almost an hour away from everyone we know and love. The distance has made it even more isolating, but this is what we could afford. The city is too expensive.

To get anywhere, we have to drive on the freeways. They are so crowded, traffic in every direction. Any trip away from home grates on my nerves—knuckles white on the steering wheel, praying the baby won't cry, blasting kids' music to drown out the sound of speeding cars or honking pile-ups. Still, we managed to drive to my parents' house once or twice a week to get help with childcare. It was far, but worth it. Their help gave me the little bit of space I needed to not completely go nuts. My husband's mom helps once in a while too, but she still works full-time, so it is much less. The hole in our support system that has been left by my parent's move is gaping.

My parents lived in the same house my whole life, in a quiet, spacious suburb. I grew up in that big home surrounded by brush-filled canyons with a huge backyard, fruit trees and vegetable gardens, a sandbox, and a jungle gym that was turned into a basketball court when my brother got older.

As a new family, we can't afford a sprawling backyard and a rich neighborhood right now, like we both grew up with. Our house is small. Our backyard is tiny. Our neighborhood is old but friendly. Every house looks the same. Some have lawns—ours doesn't, unless you count the rectangle of astroturf surrounded by gravel that sits next to our driveway. We plop ourselves down there on hot afternoons once the shade rolls in and play with the rocks. It's usually just me and my daughter. She's a toddler. Her dad works late. She doesn't have siblings. I'll never have another kid.

My parents were friends with all our neighbors. Summers meant barbecues next door with everyone on the street, riding bikes with friends until sunset, pool parties, lots of people. We only know one neighbor here: the guy next door. He's kind but kooky, helps us out when we need to borrow something but drinks a lot in his garage. Everyone else on our street is anonymous to us. It's so temporary, we haven't planted real roots.

We rent this place. My parents owned their home, took pride in it, took care of it. They carved a place for themselves to belong and raise their kids. A stable, beautiful place. But we all flew the coop years ago. So this year they finally decided to leave their familiar neighborhood for the great unknown. They sold the house and moved to Oregon in May—it's September now. I miss them. My daughter misses them. We need them, so we're moving too.

It's very different in Central Oregon—snowy, cold, and mountainy with big nature. Instead of six months of summer like we have here, it will be six months of winter. I'm afraid of the change, but I also welcome it. I'm scared and exhilarated. This could be our chance to have real community; to forge friendships that last; to have fresh water and running streams that nourish us; to create a place to truly belong.

———

To be honest, I am too tired to really think about our move. It's one foot in front of the other, one step at a time. Right now, my task is to calm the fuck down so I can keep going with my motherhood duties without having a panic attack this week.

"Oh, just do some meditation or yoga. Create a routine. Take care of yourself," my inner critic harps. I don't know why, but it's not that easy. I do meditate sometimes; I do some stretching. I go on long walks in the dry eucalyptus groves and bouldery hills near our house. It all helps a little.

But as a mother, I find myself often neglecting my own internal experience until it's too late. Then, it's so hard to sit with all the suppressed feelings once I finally have time. It's too much, too many, too tense and heartachy—I end up having a panic attack or numbing myself. I used to drink or smoke weed to hide from the overwhelm, but I don't do that anymore. Now I watch a show or read a book or think about stuff until I get disgusted and go to sleep in a ball of tension, wrapped around the unfelt feelings in my gut, cuddling them like a comfort toy in an uncomfortable way.

———

I'm sipping some cold brew with coconut milk, no ice. My curly brown hair is knotted in a high messy bun. My baggy gray sweater matches the bags under my eyes. My daughter is at home with a babysitter.

This morning, I finally spent some time unwinding the tension in my belly, letting my digestion start working on its own. I put Elmo on the TV and dumped my kid in front of it, then retreated to my room with the door cracked open. I laid down on my back and finally forced myself to move and feel. My belly creaked and gurgled. After several minutes my fight or flight mechanism turned off after days and my pipes finally started moving.

My husband also helped me today. My dear, sweet, sometimes clueless but always good-intentioned husband. He noticed my struggle this morning and did his best to help me relax. Soft touches, long hugs, grounding pressure on my legs and feet, listening to my long list of complaints and erratic emotions. It did help to have him there with me before he went to work in his home office. I was really grateful, but then I got angry at him. I picked a fight and pushed him away. I scowled and ran and cried in my car and then came back and got mad at him some more. I need to get away from him, too. It's not just my kid. But I also don't want to get away from either of them. It's a strange thing. Maybe I just want to get away from myself—this self I am being, this self that neglects herself to the point that she can't help herself and needs help and then gets mad at the people who try to help her.

———

I do have a therapist. I see her every other week. We've been working together for almost four years. I don't get mad at her for trying to help me. I look forward to our sessions. She has supported me to heal trauma, to process anger, to sit in sadness. She has been a kind and listening ear, a helpful ally. But now that I'm a mom, it isn't enough. The depression comes. The anxiety mounts. The anger flashes. The irritation grows and grows and I can't think of anything to do besides run away and scream.

I've tried medication for depression in the past. It worked for a bit but always came with heavy side effects, so eventually, I'd stop. I went on anxiety medication postpartum when things got really bad, but it only made it worse. I stopped after a week. Then I tried meditation. That helped. Then I got sober. That helped too. But eventually, the stress of life crashed back in and all my new healthy coping mechanisms weren't enough anymore.

———

Here at the coffee shop, everyone is in their own little bubble—strangers all sitting one stool apart, staring out the window or looking at their devices. Everyone is just trying to be alone, together. That's what I want. I don't want to be totally alone, but I don't want to listen or pay attention to anyone else. I don't want to go out deep into the woods all by myself and sit there listening to my own thoughts repeating in my head. My body would get all tense and worried because when I am alone, I am vulnerable. No one would hear me scream if a person or a bear or a snake or a big huge bug attacked me. I might die and no one would know; no one could help.

If there are people around, I feel safe. I also feel annoyed. I hate their sounds, their smells, their needs and wants and desires and incessant talking and thinking and attention-taking. I need them but can't stand them when I'm pent up like this—all their breathing and slurping and what the fuck.

Let's all just be quiet. I want to be alone together, safe but isolated, secure but not needed.

NO!

The moment I open my eyes, needs.
The second my feet hit the floor, "Mama!"
The minute I sit on the toilet, "Honey, where is my..."

I am wearing a coat of frustration—
nerves tight, body tense,
jaw clenched.

My skin is itching,
arms are twitching with
the impulse to flail and hit.

With every ask, every want,
every demand of my time—
the scream inside grows.

Their sounds are grating,
their needs—infuriating.
What about me?

I am constricted and flaming—
ready to combust or implode.
My eyes are blazing, mind is racing.

Temper glowing red hot,
sizzling under my thin veneer,
fuze getting shorter with every

"Mama, I want!"
"Mama, I need!"
"Honey, can you please..."

...NO!

stay

I have a habit of running away. Maybe it's more of a wound than a habit. Maybe it's a trauma response. Maybe my fight or flight gets too activated for too long and my primal brain makes me bolt. Perhaps it's just my Sagittarian nature, or something deeper, unknown.

Whatever the reason, I spent most of my twenties after college on the road, shifting from this place to that, leaving lovers or jobs, houses or communities. Whatever seemed too hard or boring, eventually I'd quit. I'd leave. I'd get up and go off in search of something greener. It was usually great when I got there, until my inner struggles caught up with me, made me itch with angst, and propelled me to leave once more.

For several years I bounced between trying to live a fun and adventurous life in the San Francisco Bay Area, living on the road in my car in Northern California and Oregon, and living at home with my parents in San Diego.

I'd try to make my way in the big city, find a job or some gigs, create a little business for myself. I'd live in a house with some people or move in with a lover for a while. I'd go dancing three nights a week, get invited to all-night psychedelic mansion parties in Marin. I was rich in relationships and explored many shapes of polyamory—dating couples, having multiple serious boyfriends at a time, being part of a strange and confusing haram of sorts. I fell in love and out of it. I broke hearts and my heart was broken. I found deep friendships—some that I still cultivate to this day, some that I've let go of along the way. It was a good life up there in the Bay.

But eventually, I'd get sick of it—tired of the grind, tired of working so much, tired of my living situation, bored of my boyfriend, hurt too badly from the latest polyamory chronicles that I couldn't stand to stay. I'd create some reason to quit or leave and not have a plan. Sometimes it wasn't my fault—I'd lose my sublease or my gig would fall through, and I didn't have a safety net besides mom and dad or my credit card, which I totally maxed out. Usually, I'd become homeless and broke and then I'd go knocking on my parent's stable door. They'd always take me in with looks of pity and love.

It wasn't always bad to be without a house or money. I never spent a night on the street. I had a car that I lived out of. I had friends' houses to stay at. Several times, I joined up with a nomadic group of van lifers that roamed from hot springs to festivals all summer. I had many magical, incredible experiences. I lived life from the perspective of being "in the flow," of following the serendipities, of allowing space for spontaneity and magic. There were beautiful moments, incredible miracles, indescribable beauty.

It was amazing and fun, until it wasn't. Until I got sick

or hurt or so run down I couldn't even work the odd jobs coming my way. Then I'd run home to my parents. They'd try to get me on my feet, offer me a place to live, a job, food, a shower, some kind of stability...and then when it all got to be too much, I'd leave again and the cycle continued. I did this several times in my twenties, maybe three or four, until a few years ago I finally stayed.

That's the time I stopped running. That's when I got humble, worked a stable restaurant job, got some real psychiatric help, and eventually created a solid business for myself. After that, I started working consistently as a healer and teacher for others, wrote my first book (that I still haven't published), finally prioritized my career path and creative work, and found real happiness and fulfillment.

That's also when I saw the error of my ways—the harm I'd caused by always leaving. I not only hurt others in all those mad dashes, but I also hurt myself. The pain I'd inflicted on myself over the years of forgoing stability to chase my fleeting impulses was huge. I had decimated my roots, chopped off my feet. I was in both financial and emotional ruin. I had no foundation. I had racked up immense debt, too much to pay back. I had severed my ties with too many people too many times. I had reinforced in my brain pathways that the world was not a safe place for me; that I would always fail; that I would never belong.

———

It was a long road to healing, but I did it. No matter how hard and uncomfortable it was, I kept showing up to my restaurant job, going to therapy, taking my medication, making amends. Slowly I got stronger, healthier, happier.

I found some sense of self-worth again and a trust in the goodness of life. From there, I started my healing and coaching business using the skills I'd gained from many holistic trainings and failed start-ups over the years.

I found my place as a leader in our San Diego community, combining my passions for movement, energy, and vulnerable relating into workshops, sessions, classes. I started building a client base, making real money, developing a sense of empowerment I had been lacking all those years of leaving. I felt good, alive, finally on track. Though I was still living with my parents, I was saving money to move out, scaling my business, expanding my influence, becoming the healer and entrepreneur I always had the potential to be.

Then, I met my now-husband. A year later, I was pregnant. We got married, had the baby, and I kept staying.

Somehow, I didn't leave, even when the going got tough. Even when our relationship was on the rocks. Even when I almost drowned in my emotions postpartum. Even when I had to give up my business and the identity I had built around it after becoming a mother because I couldn't juggle it all.

Yes, I stayed. But the urge, the wound, the tickle in my belly, the stampede of horses in my feet, the desire to run and run and never look back was there. It's here. It never went away—I just stopped acting on it. I guess that's some progress.

I'm not going to run away. But the fantasy of leaving my family and wandering off by myself into the great mysterious world with no responsibilities is tempting. Of course, this is a myth. It wouldn't be like that. It wouldn't be some grand adventure, some final freedom from my shackles. It would be hard, too, and it would hurt me like it did before.

So, when things get too tough, when my whole body is screaming at me to hit the road and not look back, still I stay. Sure, I have panic attacks sometimes, or I dissociate, or I lose myself in fantasy novels or binge-watch TV shows. But I don't leave.

The truth is, it wouldn't be a clean break. I would look back. I'd look in the mirror and think about what I ditched. Not a job or a community or a boring relationship—a daughter. A person who needs me more than she needs anyone, more than anyone has ever needed me. And if I'm honest with myself, I need her, too. I love her so much, more than I ever knew possible. She is a part of me now, an inseparable part. So I stay. It's the most excruciating thing at times, but still, I stay.

not my dream

I never wanted to be a mom. At least, I can't remember a time that I did. Actually there was that one time when I was twenty-seven. I thought about it for a month and then discarded it. I was dating a much older man and had some serious daddy issues. He was literally the same age as my parents. I think I was trying to trap him, to find a way to make him stay and care for me forever, like a good daddy. Once I revealed that I was thinking about a baby with him, he said absolutely not and shut down the fantasy. We broke up shortly after and he got a vasectomy a few months later. It was all for the best.

Looking back at my childhood, memories are foggy, few and far between. I honestly don't have much material to draw from. I remember big events, playing in the sandbox with my siblings, watching TV as a family, eating popcorn on Friday nights. I remember going to church and dance classes, playing with my neighborhood friends. I remember bits and pieces of school, feeling scared while my parents were fighting, that one time there was a huge earthquake in the middle of the night and our whole family took shelter under the kitchen table. But I have no memories of dreaming of motherhood.

At a certain age, maybe in high school, I took on the narrative that I would never get married or have children. Maybe it was true desire, or maybe it was a reaction to what I saw at home. My mom had big plans and dreams for her life, but once she got married and had children, she abandoned them and instead became a stay-at-home mom. Our childhoods were richer for it, and I'm grateful to her now. But at the time, I hated and rejected this. I wanted something more for my life. I wanted adventure. I wanted independence. I wanted to be a writer. I wanted to be the cool aunt that traveled to Europe and had tattoos.

I do have a few tattoos and I have been to Europe, but my visions of a life of freedom never panned out as entirely positive. Having this kid, getting married, choosing to stay—these have all created growth in me in ways I didn't expect. I have more integrity now. I understand responsibility. I still have been able to become a writer. But I am not free, and I'm not an aunt, yet.

I never even liked kids when I was younger. I had a strong aversion to them, in fact. I thought they were messy, loud, strange. I felt awkward around them, like they could see into my soul and knew I was bad at the core.

I always thought I'd have an abortion if I got pregnant. Somehow, I never did get pregnant until this time. Even with all my risky behavior, promiscuity, unprotected sex— I dodged that bullet.

Something changed in me when I found out I was pregnant, though. It felt right. It felt magical. It felt like destiny. I still took a week to think about it, to deliberate, to weigh the pros and cons. I can't explain why, exactly, but even though we weren't married, even though we had only been together for ten months, even though we had no financial stability or experience with long-term commitments, my boyfriend and I decided to keep it, to raise the child together, to get married and do the whole thing.

Out of nine siblings on both sides, our daughter is the only grandkid so far. This makes her incredibly spoiled. Her grandparents buy her everything: toys, clothes, furniture. I'm not complaining. We don't have much money right now, so it's really helpful and generous.

My husband and I are both the oldest children. Him: the Golden Child. Me: the Troubled One. But despite it all—the rebellion, the drugs, the running away, the resistance...I've found myself in the stable life of domesticity and motherhood.

There are terrible moments and there are beautiful ones. I relish the times we are a little happy family. We go on walks together, my husband and I stepping in stride as he pushes the stroller and we take in the fresh air. We go on bike rides around the neighborhood, the little one strapped to the front of my cruiser, husband peddling ahead, leading the way, stopping to gather mulberries and figs from the neighborhood trees. We enjoy dinners together, eating the gourmet deliciousness I concoct in the kitchen, our child shoving simple finger foods into her mouth, making a mess of her face. I smile at bath time when I sometimes sit in the warm water with her, straddling her little body while she splashes and plays with her toys, my husband beaming at the edge of the tub. I laugh when my husband strums the guitar and we sing silly songs as she dances and goofs around. There are simple, incredible, sweet moments. But I never wanted this.

I didn't dream of being a housewife. I despised it. I didn't fantasize about my wedding day. We rushed it once I decided to keep the baby, got married in my parent's backyard a few weeks later. Only ten people attended and I bought a cheap and simple floral dress from a big box store. It all happened so fast, I didn't have a chance to rationalize it. It was all emotion, all impulse, all hormones and pheromones.

Sometimes I think I made a huge mistake. Like when I'm so stressed out that I just cry my eyes out in bed, unable to do simple tasks. Like when I'm so overwhelmed that the thought of another day sends me into a hyper-ventilating panic attack. Like when I get so infuriated with my baby for not sleeping for the fifth night in a row that I want to throw her against the wall. Like when I can't stand the sight or sound or smell of my husband and push him away with anger and disgust.

This wasn't my dream, but it is my reality. I'm trying my best to find a way to make it my own, to embrace it, to love it even. Yet, I can't. Not yet. I feel so far away from myself, swamped with all the to-do's and other people's needs. I don't even know what my "self" is anymore, or where to find it.

I can't help but imagine what life would be like if I had made a different choice, not had the baby, chosen myself and my career over this life of endless duty. Maybe I would have been happier, maybe not. Maybe things would have continued to work out with my business and I would have found deeper stability, would have kept rising in mental and physical health. But maybe not. Maybe I would have run away again, ruined everything I'd worked for, because I could. Because there was nothing tying me down, no reason to stay.

Even though I find myself in a totally different reality than I ever imagined, I'm better for it in a lot of ways. Maybe this whole unexpected entanglement is exactly what I needed to become a healthier version of me. Maybe it's leading to more happiness than I ever could have had being the crazy single aunt. Right now, though, it's hard. It's endless. It's painful and it's dull. It's stressful and consuming. My daughter is almost two and I still stop sometimes and think, "What the hell did I do?"

new life

I lumbered awkwardly out of the bathroom, big mesh diaper strapped on under my purple robe, slippers on my feet. I sat down in the clunky wheelchair as the attendant held it steady. My bag was all packed. My husband picked up our two-day-old daughter from the plastic hospital crib and gently placed her in my arms. I felt my insides tremor a little.

"Ready?" the random nurse guy asked.

"Mmmhmm." I gave a small smile with pursed lips. He wheeled us out of the room, my husband following close behind, duffle bag over his shoulder.

We got in the elevator and rode in silence. The floors dinged by as we went down. My hospital room had a nice view of the San Diego mid-town area. We were five floors up, I think. After two nights in the care of nurses, we were heading home with our brand new baby.

I was in a daze, pumped full of every possible hormone. Oxytocin surged in me as I held my baby tight, cortisol and adrenaline lingering in my system from the stressful birth and past few sleepless nights with a newborn. My body felt slack and deflated like a flesh balloon. My labia was torn and hurt as I sat upright for the first time since giving birth, preferring to stay slightly reclined or fully flat in my high-tech bed with the beeps and buttons.

My husband had stayed overnight with me in the hospital. They gave us a room with two small single beds. The baby had her own see-through plastic cage between us. It was all strange, sterile, foreign. Even my own body felt like a weird place. I hated it. But I loved the smell of my baby's head, the feel of her soft body on my naked chest, the way she instinctively knew how to suckle my breast. Pride and dread danced in me.

The elevator doors opened and we coasted out. I could feel people's eyes on me, the little coo's and aw's they made as I was wheeled past them with this tiny pink person in my arms. I felt my energy wrap around her like a protective shield as we made the long trek across the sprawling lobby to the big glass front doors.

When we got out, my husband left us in front of the sliding doors and ran quickly to get the car from the parking garage. I sat in the gentle fall sunshine, hospital goers whizzing past, the attendant holding the chair handles behind me. We were silent for a few moments, then he made some small talk. I don't remember what he said. The energy of the world outside was overwhelming. Cars, horns, people, traffic. It felt too harsh for someone who had just given birth in such a traumatic way. It felt too dangerous for the helpless being in my arms.

"Are you excited to get her home?" he asked.

I paused for a moment, sorting through the mixed

feelings bubbling inside me. Excitement, terror, exhaustion, confusion, worry, happiness, sadness.

"Well, honestly, I have no idea what I'm doing," I replied a full minute later with a shrug, searching for my husband's car in the line emerging from the garage. I think the guy laughed. I'm not sure. I looked down at my baby, so fresh and new, so innocent and helpless, so utterly dependent on me for survival. A wave of fear surged through me.

Just then, a lady with a tiny dog walked by in matching pink sweaters. The carefully groomed dog even had pink shoes. It was obviously an important part of her family— her child. The irony of it weighed against the bundle in my arms and the panic in my heart. I smiled to myself, chuckled softly. "I should have just gotten a dog," I blurted.

a different way

I don't want to be seen. I don't want to be looked at or judged or pitied. I'm on edge. I'm revved up. My introvert needs are not being met in this motherly lifestyle and it's starting to really take its toll.

I try to create space for myself, create times when I am not available, go to places where the demands and noises of my family cannot be heard. I try to create boundaries around my privacy and space. It often does not work. I get interrupted anyway, or I feel guilty. Deep inside somewhere, I think I'm not supposed to have them, these needs, not allowed to create boundaries. I should be available all the time. That's what a good mother is, right?

I am chronically over-stimulated, on the verge of panic-level anxiety. I have suppressed my rage over my boundaries constantly being crossed and my needs not being met. I have shoved it down and swallowed it, like I was taught to. Like a "good woman" should. But I am not a good woman. I am a wild thing. I am a sorcerous, a magical being, an artist, a channel. I am trying to be a mother even though I never wanted to. I am trying to be a wife even though I always thought it wasn't for me. I am not doing well enough. I am not selfless enough. I am not happy enough in this narrow role. I don't think I will ever be.

I need to have my own life, my own thoughts, my own visions. I need to have space to allow the universe to speak through me, to allow creativity to bubble to the surface. I need to be able to have boundaries and not feel like a bad person because of it. I need to prioritize and take care of myself in order to be able to show up for my family.

I have been socialized by generations of female oppression to know what a good mother is. She's a martyr. She is selfless to the point of abandoning herself. She must put everyone's needs before her own. That's what a mom should be. That's what the world has taught me.

I have also been brainwashed by social media to think I know what a perfect mom is in the modern world. These hippie, new-age Instagram moms inundate my screen with photos of breastfeeding 'til their kids are five or whatever, co-sleeping peacefully, staying home and quitting their jobs joyfully, or running their businesses while raising kids with total ease and smiles. They barely use screen-time, make their own organic baby food, and never, ever give them sugar. These composites of unattainable goals are torture devices I measure myself against.

I will never be a good woman in the eyes of the patriarchy, in the eyes of the perfect new-age moms. I am not built to sustain this endless service and self-sacrifice. I stopped breastfeeding at nine months and barely regretted it. I co-slept for three weeks and then said "fuck that." I need space for myself, breathing room, interests and goals beyond the home. I'm not a happy housewife. I am something so much more, something I can almost feel and taste and see when I get enough time alone.

I am here to forge a different way, but I don't know how. It's too heavy, deep, entrenched. It's in my bones and my DNA. It's passed on from my ancestors and torments me from my phone screen. It's in our collective psyche, in our language. We applaud women for being selfless, we honor them for their endless sacrifice.

I will never be that type of woman. I am a good mother, though, and a good wife. I love them both, my baby and my husband, and my love nurtures them. I show up every day, though some days I am more present than others. I give of myself, my time, my energy. I play with them and cook for them and hold them when they need emotional care. I plan the things and do the stuff. It feels like not enough. Something in me says I should give more, do more, be more available. I shouldn't have these crazy needs for space; I shouldn't want to get away.

———

I grew up as a feminist. As soon as I knew what that was, I identified with it. I learned about the feminist movements. I could see the oppression, the inequality— and yet I grew up feeling quite equal. My upper-middle-class mostly white school in the suburbs was a bubble of gender equality. When I got to college, a teacher asked our class who identified as a feminist. I was the only one to raise my hand. In a class of thirty students, most of whom were women, I was the only one. I was shocked, appalled, ignited into action.

I've held that torch in my life—that spark of rebellious righteousness. I know women are meant for much more than lives of servitude. We have wells of wisdom within us, creative solutions for a world in peril. We need to be free to express ourselves; to liberate the truths and the great works within us. Domestic life squelches that.

Even though I grew up in a feminist reality, once I became a mother, a heavy coat of eons of pain and cultural expectations descended upon me. Now I have to sort through it and take it off piece by piece in order to have peace. My soul is bigger than the halls of this house. I have to find a way to live my truth. I have to live a life beyond domesticity. And I have to keep being a mom and a wife in a way that actually works for me, not in this old inherited soup of guilt and oppressive expectations; not in this endless comparison and failure.

———

I am too over-burdened by the weight of it—the all-the-time care-taking. I don't know how to carve enough space for myself, truly find my soul again, and create something of value in the world from within this home life. And do I deserve that? Do I get to have that?

I've been through this before. I've already done this. I've struggled with motherhood and realized I have to create a life for myself beyond this home. I published a book about my first year postpartum and started a business and found empowerment within the confines of domestic duty. But here I am again, on another arm of the spiral, defeated.

I am a highly sensitive person. I am not just a normal lady. I have anxiety. I experience depression. I am psychic.

I'm a healer, a feeler, an artist by nature. I see things and hear things and know things. I'm an introvert. I need space and time to center myself. I get overwhelmed and need to rest a lot. That's just how I am. I've always been this way. I have plenty of practices I've learned through the years to help me navigate my unique composition. I've worked as a healer, a coach, a group facilitator, a medium. I have done so much in my life and now I feel dejected. I can't muster the strength and conviction to lead, to help, to heal anyone—not even myself.

After I published my first book, I felt high and rode that as far as I could. I felt a level of stability come in from that accomplishment. I thought I had figured it out. I started writing, speaking and teaching about "maternal mental health," about "prioritizing creativity" and your own "well-being," taking time for "deep self-care" to truly feel "healthy and happy in motherhood."

Then I came down from the high and crashed into burnout. I couldn't sustain it. It wasn't true. I did not know what I was talking about. I didn't have enough time or energy to take care of myself, run a business and be a mom. I didn't have enough help. I didn't have enough stamina. It wrecked me.

I was no longer mentally healthy or stable. I quit, retreated to the hearth, tried to find fulfillment in my domestic duties. It sort of worked, but not really. The dissatisfaction was there, along with defeat. Hopelessness set in. I surrendered to that heaviness for a while, that sleepy resignation. But now, the desire to do more with my life is awake again and my insatiable need to be something other than just a mom is clawing at my belly, begging to come out. In order to do that, I need more time.

I need more space. I need more boundaries. I need to be okay with having needs and not make that mean I'm a bad mom.

Even though I feel like I can't handle anything right now, I don't want to escape motherhood altogether. There are beautiful moments. There is wonderful joy. There is laughter and astonishment. There are deep stretches of communion, of rightness, of peace—but less and less lately. This divide within me—the mother and the artist, the wife and the feminist, the good woman and the rebel—is exhausting. I have to find a way to unite them or I will be torn apart.

I am trying my best to find myself within this domestic life. I am taking steps towards my needs, learning how to create boundaries even if they seem harsh. I have to do it to be sane. I have to find a way to carve out more space and time for myself. I have to let go of all this bullshit comparison and be okay with my choices and needs. I need to make and do and build something that feels worthwhile besides dinner and child-care and legos. I have to accept that I'm different than the idealized mother archetype and create my own way. I have to trust that taking care of myself and following my desires is actually the best way I can care for everyone else. In fact, it is the only way for me.

Metal Head

Someone is screaming in my head.
No, something is screaming,
   grating,
      smashing.

It's rushing in like the ocean, loud
   like metal crashing,
      flooding my brain.

I will it to stop, to leave me be
but it keeps going on in a sea of

clashing,
   smashing,
      clanking,
         flanking,
            unrelenting
               mental noise.

swamped

Things are getting worse. I got so clear, felt so sure of what I needed to do. Then life swamped me again. I haven't picked up a pen in weeks. I haven't had time to think. I've been cooking, cleaning, caring for my kid and crying. It's so hot outside, unbearable. It's late September in Escondido and it's around 100 degrees every day.

We are trapped in the house all day long. Her little cheeks get so red when we go anywhere in the heat. I don't want to take her out until after five PM. When the sun starts to go down, I push her in the stroller on a walk around the neighborhood, trying to breathe the cooling evening air, trying to get some relief from the endlessness of our inside reality. Sometimes I take her to the mall in the middle of the day and push her around the air-conditioned halls, not buying anything. We eat lunch in the food court and I let her crawl around the dirty, germ-filled indoor play area. I stay there as long as possible, until she starts fussing, then brave the heat of the parking lot to our roasting car and drive back to this little house.

My husband is working overtime, trying to build his business, trying to generate more money for us so we can have a better life, so we can afford more child-care, so we can move to Oregon next month and have the support of my parents again. I am grateful for this—for his hard work, for his sacrifice. But I am sacrificing a lot, too. Too much. I don't have enough time. I don't have enough energy. I don't have enough help. I don't have enough patience. I don't have enough strength for this.

I'm irritable all the time. I break down often. I'm stressed beyond my capacity. I don't want to do this. I need something different than this endless childrearing in isolation. I can't live like this.

Because of my large need for space and my sensitive nervous system, my husband and I have created as much distance for ourselves as possible under one little roof. We share the master bedroom, technically, but I also inhabit the guest room, which I have turned into my bedroom and office. Not much work gets done in there lately, but at least it's a step in the right direction. Sometimes I get a break to be in there when he has an hour or two to be with our daughter and I retreat. Granted, it's the room right in the middle of the house, surrounded by the kitchen, the living room, and the other bedrooms, so when anyone is home and awake there is very little sound privacy. Even if I'm taking time for myself, door shut, headphones on, I'm still alert, anticipating a knock or a loud sound or a barging in. I'm there, deep in restful meditation, finally calm and able to ground my nervous system, then BAM, the kitchen cabinet slams shut and I startle to attention. Or I'm doing some yoga, finally feeling my body, stretching out these tightly held frustrations, and my daughter gets away from my husband somehow and pounds at the door, "Mama, Mama..."

His home office is in the garage, which works pretty well. Even though it's hot and sweaty out there, he endures it to give us space during the day so we don't hear his client calls and typing sounds.

Our almost-two-year-old daughter has her own bedroom and bathroom. It's a small house, but at least we have our own little spaces and are not totally on top of each other. We are lucky in that way, I guess.

My room is decorated with purples and maroons, crystals and twinkle lights, icons and artwork of goddesses and affirmations. It's my little sanctuary space, complete with an electric piano and a funky antique lamp. It's a space where I can try to figure out who I am now.

This seems nearly impossible, though. Even with the years passing us by, I still can't quite find the time to discover myself in this new reality. I have too many responsibilities and not enough reprieve. I want to be completely isolated in a nirvana-like state of just me and my things for a while. I crave that so deeply, so purely, so completely, it makes me cry.

In one week, my husband is traveling to be a groomsman in a wedding. I was going to go, too. We made plans for our daughter to stay with my parents for five days while we traveled together. They are coming to visit from Oregon for a week, staying at a beach condo. With all this going on in me, I decided today that I will stay here. He can go and have fun with his college friends. Our kid can go have a good time with grandma at the ocean. I am going to stay home. Here. Alone.

I am going to be with myself. I'm going to claim that

space and bask in it. I am going to feel myself and love myself. This will be the most time alone I've had since I became a mom. I am going to take it. I am going to heal.

part 2

TIME ALONE

goodbye for now

I turned off the engine and took out the key. My daughter was still singing some baby song in the back seat, words half-formed. I opened the door, planted one foot then the other on the concrete of the parking garage, walked around to the passenger side and unbuckled her car seat.

"You will have so much fun with Yiayia," I cooed as I lifted my daughter from her harness. I placed her gingerly on my hip and kissed her sweet, fragrant head. I hugged her close to me, savoring the feel of her body. We walked out of the parking garage and towards the condo where my parents were staying.

"Yiayia!" she squealed as she saw her grandma come out the door. It had been six months since they'd seen each other, an eternity in baby years. I put her down gently and she waddled over to hug her grandmother's legs, laughing. My mom picked her up and embraced her deeply. "I missed you so much!" She beamed, excited to spend time with her only grandchild. "You're here to sleep over at

Yiayia's vacation house!"

I left them at the door and walked back into the parking garage, opened the trunk, pulled out a duffle bag of her things, slammed the door shut, trudged back to the condo. We all walked inside, duffle slung over my shoulder—full of baby clothes, diapers, toys, and the stuffed animal she sleeps with. I set it down in the living room next to the long stretch of glass doors facing the uninterrupted ocean view. After taking in the sight of the sea, I hugged my mom and thanked her for the generous offer to watch my daughter for five whole days. "No problem," she smiled, eyes glimmering. I know she missed the little one. It was the longest she'd been away from her granddaughter since birth. Maybe she missed me, too, but likely less. I was old news. Whatever.

After some niceties and logistics, I made my way to the door to leave. My daughter was fully engrossed in playing with the toys I had brought for her. My dad was out somewhere, would be back later. The condo smelled of ocean air, potpourri, and bathroom cleaner, just as it had when we stayed there multiple times over the years, both with our kid and without. The condo belongs to my husband's family, a permanent vacation spot for anyone who wants a beach getaway. The decor always changed, from shag carpets to teal blue nautical themes, whatever was most in fashion. This time it was decked out in navy, with tasteful ocean artwork on the walls.

I said goodbye to my daughter, kissed her on the head. I told her to be a good girl for her grandma, and that I'd see her again really soon. She smiled and went back to playing with her toys. My mom hugged me at the door, told me to have a good time. I never told them I wasn't going to the wedding. Somehow, I thought if I revealed I was staying home alone, I'd lose my chance. They'd decide not to come, realizing it wasn't a necessity. But it is a necessity. I have a deep and dire need to be alone or surely I will die.

I didn't cry any tears when I left. I'd see my kid again too soon. She would be fine. Her grandparents are great caregivers. She loves them. It's all good.

I got in the car, turned on the ignition, and quickly shut off the baby song coming through the speakers. With just the rattle of the engine humming in the background, I sighed. I sighed again and again. Then I did cry. Not because I was scared to leave my baby. Not because I would miss her like crazy. Because I was so fucking relieved.

I cried and cried in that parking garage, emptying myself of years of stress. Eventually, I stopped, blew my nose, wiped my eyes, shifted to reverse, pulled out of the parking spot, and drove out of the garage. I opened the windows, letting the ocean air blow through my hair. I breathed deep, deeper than I had in a long time, taking in the smell of it, the salt and sand and car exhaust. I merged onto the highway and stepped on the gas, driving faster than necessary. I sighed again and again, my body finally releasing all that tension. My husband was gone, had left that morning for the wedding. My kid was in safe hands, away from me. I was driving down the freeway, truly free for the first time since giving birth. Wind in my hair, air in my lungs, I cackled loudly and sped towards my empty house.

in the beginning

I laid in my big king-size bed all alone with no shirt on. It was two weeks after I gave birth. My body was a mess, all flab and lumps, still leaking blood into my adult diaper. My mind was foggy, heavy, empty.

My parents were downstairs with the baby. We were living with them for a few months. The TV was on. I could hear whispers of some home renovation show drifting up the stairs and under the crack in my door.

My mind was dull and fuzzy. Very few thoughts floated in and out. I turned my head to the side and stared at the sunlight coming through the slats of the almost-closed blinds.

My husband was at work, had just returned to his retail job selling mattresses. He hadn't started his own business yet. The bedside table was littered with tea cups, empty plates with crumbs on them, tissues, nipple balm. I was still on bed rest.

I was tired. So tired. So tired I couldn't even think about how tired I was. The whole thing was completely overwhelming: short naps in between feedings, holding a baby all day and night, barely able to stand up by myself, rips in my most tender place still gaping, healing.

I needed to sleep while my parents were taking care of my kid. I had to rest, to recharge before another day and week and years of caring for this creature that emerged from my womb. I couldn't. My eyes fluttered open and closed, open and closed, but sleep didn't come.

I turned my head to the center, looked down at my bulging belly. I turned my head to the other side, stared at my own eyes in the mirrored closet door. I didn't recognize myself. Big cheeks, red eyes, puffy, vacant. Finally I was alone, but I wasn't happy. I wasn't anything. I was empty and lost.

This was the second day in a row I had asked for a stretch of alone time. The first two weeks of being a mom had been sweet for the most part. I was in a bubble of oxytocin and awe. I stared down at my tiny baby and gently stroked her head, amazed. But now, it was wearing off and reality was setting in. I didn't want visitors. I didn't take phone calls. My cell was on silent, face down. I needed some space from the child, from everyone. I needed to not be touched. I needed to not be sucked on. I needed to not be needed.

I thought I would find some sense of self, some reprieve, if only I could be alone. But it didn't come. Nothing did. Nothing was there and I was nothing, too. I was a hollow shell, a place holder, a baby feeder and tender. I tried to think some original thought, grasping for my mind, but it was far away. So I just laid there, turning my head from side to side, seeing things then closing my eyes then opening them again.

An hour later, I heard a cry, then footsteps coming up the stairs. I heard a knock at my door. "Hon? She's hungry."

"Okay," I mumbled, pushing myself up from laying to reclining, still not able to sit up all the way. The door opened, my mom walked in, the baby was placed in my arms. I felt the weight of her and sighed, pulled my boob out from under the covers, and smushed it into her mouth. She started sucking, taking, needing. Alone time was over—another day going by in a blur.

Simple Luxuries

Today I woke to a quiet house
Nothingness stretched before me
I opened my eyes then closed them again
No one around to see

No one home to scream and need
I chuckled then rolled over
Wrapped myself around myself
And went back to sleep

Later when I woke again
House still quiet, my eyes smiled
Lazed around a little bit
Stretched my arms up overhead

One leg down and then another
I propped myself up and stood
Stretched again, looked at the clock
Opened the blinds and laughed

Another day all to myself
Nowhere to go, nothing to do
No one to feed or bathe or rock
No need to find that missing sock

The second hand ticked slowly on
I sauntered to the kitchen to make my brew
Boiled some water, waited blankly
In the quiet, empty place

I took a deep breath and then I sighed
Looked at my nails, touched my hair
Rubbed my eyes, scratched my thighs
And stared into space with a smile

Nothing to do, nowhere to go
No one to be, no one who needs me
I made my coffee, sat on the porch
And savored the fresh air

The simplest acts, a deep relief
The nothingness, a luxury
I take it in and find some peace
Finally, no one's around.

an adept beholder

The terra-cotta pots look beautiful in the subtle afternoon light—the kind of light where greens and brownish reds pop out and glow in fresh wonder, cleansed and nurtured by the first fall rain. I am staring out at cloudy wet perfection, sliding door open, breathing in the freshness, savoring the smell of just-soaked dry ground. Inside, the carpet houses my hours of introspection, reconnecting with the depths of my soul again. I am alone here. My family has been gone for three days. I still have two more nights to myself. It feels heavenly.

Earlier, I drank ancient tea slowly from a clay pot, pouring endless rounds of coppery perfection. The liquid was dark as soil at first and then ever lighter with each draining and refilling. After three rounds of steeping, it became a shiny copper—the same color as the clay pots outside.

Everything keeps fitting back together like an endless work of art. Sure, there are twists and hardships, utter defeat. Yet life somehow weaves back again in more astonishing ways, evolving toward ever-greater beauty.

And here is that beauty in form: independent of my efforts, just existing. Life is rhyming with itself in color and I am present enough to see it. There is the beauty and I am the beholder, making meaning out of the rust-colored pillow in the corner of the room that catches my eye, perfectly matching the hue of the tea and the pots outside. These chromatic miracles stimulate my mind and give me a gateway to all my senses with astonishing presence. After taking in the sights, I then imbibe on the swirl of scent streaming in from outside—the eucalyptus and dirt and weeds wet with the ecstasy of rainfall. It is the luxurious smell of a longtime longing fulfilled—rain, finally, after a long, hot summer.

As I take it all in, my long-time longing is also being quenched—my deep desire to enjoy these things and think my thoughts and write these words and feel the tender caress of the cool air. I can finally relax as the nature around me exhales with relief from the support that wet weather brings; the quiet house free from familial obligation allows me to sink into myself and breathe deeper, too.

I have been far away from myself, unable to clear space back to this place of wise enjoyment. There is a re-association with my senses and my body happening that I haven't felt in so long. I have been vacant since that baby was born, since I lost the ability to inhabit this vessel as my own and believe it is beautiful.

Now I gently stroke my belly and feel it rumble, then relax. Now I breathe in deep, again and again, with no agenda other than the breath itself. Now I cup my own breasts and feel their sensuality instead of their biological function. I open my hips with loving attention—instead of cursing then for being too large, instead of thinking thoughts of hate about my curves. I caress them. I bask in my body again after so long trying to change it or escape it.

———

I have not been able to be this present since becoming a mother. I have been so stressed, too stressed, stressed beyond my ability to unwind. But now, I finally have time and space. I am rehabilitating my soul and body and creativity, communing with long stretches of stillness, relaxing all the tightly held places, opening wound wounds, unraveling the years of maternal service that bound my body up in an anxious knot of not enough time to myself.

Now I'm finally getting some—five days alone. Five days to feel and heal and be still enough for the muse to return and allow my turn-on and impulses to guide me. I feel connected to who I truly am, more than ever. I am finally integrating all the lessons I've learned as a mom, entwining them with the truths I know as an artist, a witch, a woman.

I am home now in this little corner of space and time drinking tea on the floor. There is a tiny table and tiny cups and modern symphonic music surging along in the background. Occasionally, the sound grabs me in a tizzy of crescendo and then brings me back down to the earth, back to my body. I revel in the up and the down, the excitement and the integration. As I listen, everything slows down and then swells gradually to full arousal as the strings seductively guide me on an ever-inflating joy ride of sensation and emotion until it finally completes, silence.

All songs come to an end. My time in this bubble of solitary pleasure will, too. There will be a time when I am no longer enjoying a partly cloudy day, my favorite kind of day, in exactly my own kind of way. In a few days, I will no longer be doing whatever I want, communing with creativity and my own wholeness, relaxing into the sensuousness of living and breathing and seeing and hearing—of fully being alive. Life will get busy again. I will get stressed again. My responsibilities will return full-force and so will my family.

But for now, I will keep sinking into this divine moment and trust in the goodness of life, feasting on the abundance of beauty around and inside me with the eyes of an adept beholder.

finally I miss him

Finally, I have a chance to miss him. Finally, he is far enough away that I can actually see him. So close, I get smothered, can't even find the places where his cells come together in a body—it's just hot breath and painful merging of our auras all the time.

I need to be able to breathe, to move around and dance with no one watching. To lay down and do nothing without someone judging me or walking in mid-thought.

Finally, I have a chance to be bored. To not know what to do with myself. To have so many options and none of them include another person. To feel overwhelmed with my aloneness, then glad, then gleeful, then stoic, then whatever comes next without his introjection.

I need time for introspection, for the nothingness that comes before a great idea, for the feeling of counting down the hours until I sleep, only to get a second wind and have a dance party alone in my bedroom.

After all this time and struggle, I really don't know if I'm the marrying type. Maybe I am more suited to live alone in the forest, an old crone with her herbs and birds. The silence—a sanctuary.

Living with this man I call my husband has been both a blessing and an extreme challenge. That's how I would describe our entire relationship, in fact.

It wasn't love at first sight. But when we shared a hug that first night, I did feel something. I wanted to know him. As a friend. "He's too young for me," I determined. He's two years older than me.

We started as friends—going on hikes together, making music in his studio bedroom—a private unit detached from the main part of a house that he shared with two other guys. The mismatched, used-up, beat-up furniture somehow worked for him. The futon bed with holes in the foam on the floor seemed endearing but gross. It didn't matter. He was just my friend. A great friend.

He was into producing electronic music, and so was I. He was into smoking spliffs, and so was I. He was into dancing and cuddle parties, and so was I. He was into creating community events that combined the arts and connection. So was I. But still, I held back. Our friendship grew. "Just friends."

But then, a few months after we met, I saw him with his shirt off. We were in his tiny studio with no AC, doors open wide to let in a bit of breeze, early summer making us sweat. He slid past me, body glistening in the heat as I sat on a hard chair against the wall. We were making music together that day, deep in the creative flow. I saw his shirtless pecs and abs glide by and my eyes got wide. "OH!" I thought. I was attracted to him. I didn't realize it until that moment. I freaked out, looked away, didn't want to act on it. I didn't want to ruin our friendship. It was so great, so needed, so healing. I tried for a few more weeks to stifle my romantic feelings, but they won out in the end.

Eventually, our friendship turned into a kiss, a kiss turned into a make-out, a make-out turned into a date or two, which turned into a conversation about what we were becoming. He wanted to experiment with polyamory for the first time. I was in a phase of feeling completely pessimistic about it, hurt too many times, wanting to try monogamy. I won. We were a monogamous couple a month later.

It wasn't a blissful joyride, though. Our coupling was an incredibly rocky road. We both had baggage. Big time. He hadn't been in a relationship for six years, harboring emotional and sexual stuff too deep to even go there. I hid from my issues by having multiple partners and never going deep enough to fully unearth them. Ours was not an easy relationship. We had multiple ups and downs, breakups and make ups, all within the first nine months.

Around ten months, we had just gotten back together and were finding a groove. As hard as our intimacy seemed at times, it was also incredible and fulfilling. I felt seen and heard and loved. I felt the rumbling in my soul that this guy was my mate. There was something special in our bond, something unique and powerful. We really started to stabilize into that truth and hit our stride. A month later, I got pregnant. After a week of debating, I decided to keep the baby. A month after that, we got married. Looking back, it seems totally crazy. Rash. Impulsive. Not a good idea.

We are friends at the core. That truth has bound us together, given us a foundation, gotten us through the past few years of more hardship than either of us was prepared for. We have had some good times, some great adventures, some major triumphs. We're there for each other, are able to communicate well enough, share some deep and powerful moments. We are a good pair in a lot of ways and work well as a team. And also, it's been hard.

I do like him. I love him, I'm pretty sure. But going from being a polyamorous witch girl who always leaves when things get tough to a married monogamous mother who has to keep staying...has been confusing. For both of us. He has always been incredibly independent too. Neither of us is experienced with this cohabitation thing, especially not with a child and a business and financial burden and the stress. He seems to be doing a bit better with it all, but he's a more easy-going person in general.

Maybe monogamy is a mistake for us. Maybe living together with our lives completely entwined is actually hurting our relationship. Maybe I will destroy our love simply because I can't tolerate this much closeness, don't know how, never have before.

———

I don't understand how to exist like this. I need much more space. I am a caged bird. I can tolerate my cell mate but only when we are free to fly. When we are closed in like this, I want to peck his eyes out. I don't really want to do that, but they are the thing I see day in and day out—when I wake and go to sleep and often when I shit, those eyes are there. When I eat and when I shower and when I meditate and when I brush my teeth, he is there and it's all too much.

I don't know how to be loving when we are together every single day and night. With space I am able to finally see him, miss him, want to be near him, crave to connect with him. When we are so close all the time, I can't stand him. I can't remember why I like him. I can't step back and think of him fondly. He is just there and there and there again and I don't know why I married him in the first place. I don't know why marriage is any good. I don't know why I liked hanging out with him at all. When we are together every day and night, his existence makes me crazy. His chewing is so loud and makes me want to run away screaming or slam doors or smash plates or die.

———

But now, I feel gratitude. I feel fondness. I feel the joy of anticipated reunion. I feel some inkling of missing him, of curiosity, of wanting to know how he is and what he is thinking. This time alone has refreshed my perspective. I feel so lucky to have him as my partner, as my best friend, as the love of my life. I look forward to hugging and making music and making love. I am once again excited by our lives together. I don't want to kill him, not even to maim. I am finally relaxed and have space for him in here—in my heart, in my mind, in this house. The tension I've been holding for years has melted and in its place is room for him, for us, for our love.

Maybe I am the marrying type. Maybe I just need to do it a bit differently—with more space to tend to myself and spread my wings sometimes.

memory games

From this rested and relaxed place, I can see the good in my relationship, the happiness we've shared as a family, the positive qualities I have always had. When I am stressed and struggling, the past is black and bleak: our relationship has always been hard, I've never liked being a mom, I've always been a fuck-up.

Neither is the ultimate truth. Mood colors the past and contorts our memories. Reality is somewhere in between. My husband's love has healed me, helped me, grown me. He has also smothered me, annoyed me, frustrated me. My child's birth was an incredible, beautiful moment. It was also terrible, traumatic, and has haunted me ever since with feelings of failure. Becoming a mother has helped me grow roots, get stronger, become a woman of deep integrity. It has also ripped away my identity, distanced me from my passions, destroyed my sense of freedom and adventure. My relationship with my daughter is sweet and loving, deep and bonded—and it is also turbulent and distanced, infuriating and full of regrets.

When I have time and space to myself—to think and dream and unwind—I see the beauty of it all: the ways that life has helped me, cheered me on, given me so many blessings. When I'm in the thick of it, I hate it. I want to escape. I can't see any good and it all feels like a giant mistake.

From that place of wanting to run away, my wandering past feels like the glory days. I long to get back to that uninhibited freedom, that sense of magic in everyday life that I remember. When I am more grounded and content, I remember how hard it was back then, too. How troubled I was. How terrible it was to never fully feel at home and always have financial insecurity.

There are so many lenses we can use to see the past. Our mind is like a viewfinder—switching the scene to color the landscape of our memories with different moods and perspectives. The self we construct from those memories is malleable. Sometimes I was a superstar sex goddess following a trail of miracles from party to party. Sometimes I was a dejected, homeless burnout addicted to weed. Sometimes I was a bohemian artist revolutionary helping to create a new world. Sometimes I was a flaky, self-centered hippie in denial about reality.

The truth is somewhere in between—a mix of it all and none of it at the same time. This means the reality of the past is actually a mystery. So, in this quest to find myself in motherhood, I have to focus on the present. I have to let go of my romanticized memories and my critical ones. I have to leave behind the dreams I had for myself and my life back then. They no longer apply. I am someone new now.

To discover who I am and how to move forward in a good way, I have to stop ruminating and digging around in the past for answers. I have to shake it all off, shed my skins and false memories. I have to find my way to the present moment over and over again. That's the only thing that's really true. That's the only self I can know for certain.

Allowing

I am allowing creativity to speak—
stepping back to hold space
for the muse to move and think—
bringing Nothing into being,

Inviting my Spirit to
sing and dance and play the way
to prayer and appreciation,

Growing stronger with each moment
of trusting the unknown
and living into the exhilarating flow

Of not doing but allowing perfect creation
to make me do the things I'm born to do
when I get out of the way
open my mind and let it come through.

goodbye

I am sitting on a boulder at the top of a hill. It is flat and warm, smooth and ancient. I feel a relaxed hollowness in my belly. My breaths are long and deep. I notice the sun on my skin and smile. Here I am, relaxed and free. Here I am, present and happy.

I'm scribbling in the small notebook I keep in my purse. I always have pens in there too, ready to write at any moment.

It's a nice day, not too hot. I spent the last hour walking the beautiful trails behind our neighborhood. They lead up a bouldery mountain covered in sage brush and eucalyptus trees. Everything has dried out from the rain.

As I hiked, a dusty scent filled the air and brought me back to the present with a deep breath each time my mind wandered. It feels good to be outside, to move my body, to break a little sweat. It feels good to walk and walk and not be hurried, not have to get back to anything, not need to tend to anyone. I don't have to be home at any certain time. I don't have to cook dinner if I don't want to. I can just eat crackers and cheese and call it a night. I can stay out 'til the sun is going down and not worry about anyone's bedtime. I don't have to carry anyone or push a stroller or worry about administering snacks. I can walk at my own pace and be in my own thoughts and sit as long as I want. Tomorrow, though, this vacation from my motherhood reality comes to an end.

In these five days alone, I've been able to finally unwind. I've been able to process my emotions, to feel the stuck feelings, to cry the angry tears. I've walked and stretched and danced. I've stared into space and out of windows. I've meditated more deeply than I've been able to in years. I found my creative spark again. I wrote words and sang songs. I found love for myself and rested into the goodness of life. I rediscovered gratitude and grace. I looked long at my own face in the mirror and found a friend there. I let go of my furrowed brow. I bathed luxuriously with candles and soft music. I gently stroked my belly and rubbed it with oil. I ate slow meals of delicious food. I sat in restaurants and read books. I let tears fall for no reason and every reason. I hugged myself and smiled my way to sleep.

From this perspective, here and now, I'm excited for our family reunion. I'm looking forward to hugging my baby, to kissing my husband. I almost crave the togetherness. Almost.

This is my last day alone. The sky is clear and blue. My mind is spacious and full of wonder. My heart is patient and my soul recharged. I can do this. I can resume my duties. I can stay connected to this version of me while taking care of everything, I think. I want to. I want to be this kind and happy person with my family. I want to maintain this calm and creative state while we move to Oregon. I want to be this buoyant while I meet new people, forge a new life, make a new path for us in uncharted territory.

———

My husband comes back from his trip tomorrow and I will pick up my daughter from her grandparents at the beach. We'll come home and get back into the groove of life—except in a few days, it will all be turned upside down. We will enter a frenzy of packing, getting ready to move to a different state. We leave in two weeks.

Though I look forward to the tall trees and new environment, I will miss this little trail close to our house. It is desert and rocks. It is cactus and chaparral. It is eucalyptus and oaks. It is valleys and hills. It is beautiful and arid. It is dry and wonderful. It's welcoming in a harsh way I've gotten used to. This place feels like home.

Our new home will be an even more nourishing environment. It will be different and unfamiliar, but it will be more lush and inviting. In Oregon, there will be nature and rivers all around. Hopefully there will be more friends and community, too; more connection, more love.

We are taking a chance on ourselves, leaping into the unknown in hopes of finding more of what we need to feel healthy in this complex world. We need more than this dry land and this huge sprawling city can offer us. We are not meant to live in the desert. We are not meant to go it alone. We are meant to be like lush forests with roots connected. We need more people. We need more fresh air. We need more clean water and helping hands. That's why we're going.

Sitting here now I feel a wave of sadness. It suddenly feels hard to say goodbye to these parched forests and dry dust, to these people I call friends whom I barely see but still know and love. Everything in Oregon is unknown, different. The forests are bigger. The rivers are wider. The weather is colder—much, much colder. The people are new. Will they be friendly? Will we find the community we long for? I don't know. We can't know.

What I do know is that right now, I am good. I am great. I feel grounded and alive. I feel emotions arise and pass. I feel my mind wander and then re-center. I am in touch with my senses. I am inhabiting my body. I feel healthy. I feel sane.

I have to carve out more time for myself like this, more time to just be and think and breathe. More time to write and walk and create and not be interrupted. More time to find my way back to presence, to stop worrying about all the little things, to stop caretaking for a few days and take care of myself.

I don't know when I will have another chance for this much space and time. It might be years until I get a break this long again. But I will try my best to carve out little moments, little breaks, little days or nights away if I can. I know I need that.

To stay sane in motherhood, I have to tend to myself as much as I tend to others. I have to nourish my own well-being just as I nourish everyone else around me. Otherwise, I will burn out. Otherwise, I will dry out like this old empty creek bed I am sitting beside.

The sun is starting to set. The air is cooling. The smell around me is changing from dust to the luscious scent of dusk. I hear crickets somewhere cooing. It's time for me to go. Not because I have to, but because I want to. I want to go home and have one more quiet dinner. I want to run myself one more peaceful bath. I want to walk the halls of my small house, touching walls and feeling things without being interrupted. I want to bask in the stillness and then make my own noise before retiring to bed. I want to soak up this one last sweet night of freedom before the ruckus returns, before everything changes, before the stress and the hurry comes back in.

This time alone has been the greatest gift, the biggest blessing. I finally feel like I'm okay. I finally feel like I can do this. I finally don't want to run away. Being right here right now is pleasurable and sweet. Being this me in this moment is a miracle I savor.

Next week we will enter a whirlwind of packing and upheaval. Tomorrow we will return to the family dynamic. But right now it's just me for one more night and I'm going to take in every sweet, deep, peaceful breath I can.

part 3

THE THICK OF IT

back and forward

I t all came right back. The anger. The anxiety. The frustration.

I am overwhelmed.

I had a day or two of relative peace and ease and then it all returned. I had a few nights of adoring connection with my husband, a few mornings of patience and joy with my daughter, and then it was gone, as if my miraculous time alone had never happened. As if things were exactly the same, only completely different. This time, there was the added pressure of moving, and the fear. Plus packing, planning, putting everything together as neatly as possible and cramming it into a giant truck.

When I left, the house was still a ramshackle mess—things and trash and boxes everywhere. I got on a plane on my own with our almost-two-year-old and flew to a different state. By the time we got to Oregon, I was totally burnt out again. Then there was the cold, and waiting for my husband to show up five days later with the moving truck.

Luckily, we were staying at my parents' house while he drove up all our things, so I had some help with my daughter. During the breaks that my mom gave me, I mostly laid in a tiny twin bed in the guest room. I slept a lot. I shivered, cold—feverish, even. The frigid weather was hard on my body and mind. The whole ordeal knocked me out and I surrendered to depression under piles of blankets.

I tried to adventure out, to see the town, take in the sights. I did a little bit. But mostly I was weighed down, heavy, burdened by too many feelings and too much stress.

When my husband arrived, three men I had never met before showed up at our new house to help unpack. They were friends of acquaintances we had met that summer when we visited. Even through my tired eyes and blurry gaze, I knew they would be our friends. There was a certain light about them, a familiarity that shined. I found myself smiling, leaning in, hugging, opening my heart— energized. As they hurriedly unloaded our possessions from the truck and I directed where to put it all, I started to relax.

After they left, we slowly began the process of unboxing and arranging everything. It took a few days. With each possession unwrapped, each candle and table put in place, the weight gently lifted. We were home. We made it. Everything was new, fresh, strange, wonderful. The intensity of the move began to fade and joy was there. The burnout lifted, and happiness peeked through.

———

I danced around our new home one night, candles lit, music floating through the hall. Our daughter was asleep in her new room. The moon was full. My husband meditated on a cushion as I turned and whirled, pranced and wiggled my way around the space. It's a small house, not our permanent home. We are renting. Eventually we will buy something. Our neighborhood is nothing special, but it's safe. I like it. We have twinkle lights in our living room. The carpet is soft and clean. The bathtub works and I soak in it almost every night, warming my bones and my frozen toes.

It's not even winter, still fall. We missed the changing of the leaves, but there is no snow yet. Still, the cold is astounding, shocking, foreign. When we left San Diego, it was an eighty-degree day. When I arrived off the plane, it was in the mid-forties. The temperature is dropping each day. Soon the real cold will come. I don't feel ready.

Yet, there is warmth here, too. We have new friends. They came over one night for a housewarming party. We met a bunch of people when we visited here in August, and they came over to celebrate with us. One of the guys who helped us move in was there, too.

We sat in a squished circle on the floor of the living room, all ten of us. We ate chocolate and drank tea. We shared truths and sang songs. We laughed. I felt awkward but happy, self-conscious but free. This is our new community. This is our new home. This is our new life. This is my chance to integrate the old me and the new, the mother I am and the wild woman I know myself to be deep down inside. This is a new chapter, a fresh page, a new stage for our lives to unfold.

My daughter starts part-time daycare next week. I will

have four precious hours to myself, four days a week. I will have space to be alone and together, to be myself and the mother I must be—both a creator and a nurturer, a woman and a wife—all that I am, complete.

first snow

Driving down the road in the first snow of the year, tears filled my eyes. I paused at a stoplight and wept. I had never driven in snow before. This was the first time I had ever lived in a place where it snowed. While the fall in this new town felt extra crisp and I was still getting used to the nature everywhere, it had been fun and familiar enough. Now, I was way out of my element.

It wasn't fear, exactly, though fear was there. It wasn't sadness, or grief fully. It definitely wasn't total happiness, or hopefulness, or awe. It was some combination of all of those, pushing me to get excruciatingly present as the white fluffs fell and I drove my daughter home from daycare. My heart swelled and emptied out my eyeballs. I smiled and grimaced at the same time. I gripped the steering wheel while trying to stay calm. It wasn't even sticking on the ground yet. It would be okay. Even though I had never done this before, even though I have never lived in snow. I have never had to wear long underwear or boots or hats or gloves or puffer jackets on top. Even though I have never had to make sure my socks were warm enough and my shoes grippy enough. Even though everything familiar was a thousand mile away in the Southern California sunshine.

It all plowed into me, confronting me with an unfamiliar dread, an unnamable concoction of feelings that startled me into the truth: I have no idea what I'm doing.

For a San Diego native, winter is a novelty. For a central Oregonian, it's the norm. It's expected. It's anticipated. It's celebrated, even. I thought forty degrees was cold. That was nothing. Now my sinuses are dry, my hair is flat, my nose and cheeks are red, my legs are stiff from wearing so many pairs of pants and my toes are pretty much always cold. Now that it's snowing, my movement in the world is constricted, too. I'm afraid to go anywhere in my car. But this is life. Tomorrow I will have to drive out again and take my daughter to daycare across town. My little car without four-wheel drive will be put to the test—along with my driving skills—as I navigate an icy world I have never experienced before.

In some ways, it's exciting. It's a whole unknown realm of white and cold and slippery roads. I get to figure out how to move through it. I get to learn new things and sink slowly, day by day, into comfort within this unfamiliar wonderland.

But what if I don't get comfortable? What if I never like this type of life? What if I don't find good enough friends and I hate the snow forever and I want to leave? Will we move again? Will we pack up our whole lives into a huge truck and trek across the country, or even across the world, and start all over again? I don't want to do that.

I don't want to move again. I want to be home. I crave home. I crave belonging. I crave a place where I am accepted and loved and feel good and thrive. But maybe this snowy mountain town isn't it. Maybe I will go crazy by the end of winter. Maybe I will be depressed and unhappy again, like I was before. Maybe my anxiety will skyrocket from having to drive in snow and walk in snow and live in snow and cold for months. Maybe I'm out of my element more than I know, more than the weather, more than my awkward stance in this many pants. Maybe I'm in danger. Maybe I'm in for more surprises than I bargained for.

Or maybe this is the place for me. Maybe this is my home forever. Maybe I'll drive through snow every winter and have all this gear to get through the weather and deal with the cold, dry air and the flat hair and the red nose and the constant edge of fear. Or maybe I'll relax into it and love it. Maybe I'll become a snow person and this will all feel fun someday. Maybe this is the moment that I am leaning in and embracing it, letting it into my heart, letting myself feel the feelings that are in the way of this truly being home.

This all whirled through my being, mixed with the awe of nature and the power of the elements and the smallness and vulnerability of each human, myself included, and my tiny daughter, even smaller, and how big my responsibility for her is, and the fact that I don't actually know what I'm doing but I'm the one in charge, I'm the adult, and I could drive us to a snowy death one day and it would be all my fault. Or maybe it would be someone else's fault...do they all know how to drive in snow? What if they are reckless and dangerous on the icy roads, or inexperienced like me?

Can I trust all those other drivers out there?

All this flashed by in an instant in my car today, stopped at a red light with the snow gently swirling. I couldn't name it at the time but I felt it all, welling in my belly, my chest, out my tear ducts—a multilayered mix of emotions, of half-baked thoughts and barely understood feelings. It tickled and swelled and dripped from my face as kid music played and my daughter sang her baby songs streaming through the back speakers. Then the light turned green and I drove into the rest of my life.

not my days

The days are structured around her schedule: early wake-up, feedings, school for a few hours on weekdays, nap time, wake-up, snack, play, dinner, bath, story time, bed. We do this over and over every day. The few hours a day she goes to daycare speed by in a flash. I don't have time for much. It's not enough. Sure, I get a few hours to myself. I can go on walks now, I can sit and drink coffee and think, I can meet a new friend by the river for an hour. But there's still so much to do and clean and shop for and take care of. It's not all my own time. It never ends.

I put on a video for her so I can clean the kitchen in peace. After dishes and sweeping, I find myself sometimes standing around, looking for something else to clean, something else to do that is mindless enough yet feels productive. The days spent in a domestic daze make it so hard to break into a different pattern. But sometimes I do. Sometimes I am able to sit down and write, or meditate, or read something, or practice a song in between all my endless caretaking duties. I have to find ways to break out of the mundane spell and into creative inspiration. It's necessary for my sanity. I have to find respite and quiet within the screaming and crying and whining and loud noise. My sensitive system and artistic soul require special care that is hard to come by in mom life. It takes tenacity to carve it out for myself; it takes strength to switch gears in the middle of the day and create something when really my nerves are fried and I just want to tune out by watching mindless television or drinking way too much coffee and finding something else to clean.

Like just now, I was finally finding a flow state in writing. I had carved out a little pocket of time that was mine while my husband played with the baby for twenty minutes, and then I heard the dreaded sound of, "Where's Mama? Let's find her!" and next thing I know, they are marching into my quiet space with their noise and needs. So I got literally dragged out by my hand and made to sit and watch my kid play with her new toy while her dad made too-loud noises with too much enthusiasm.

Any deep thinking can be interrupted at any time without apologies, so making anything of depth is extra challenging as a mom. I don't know why I just don't say, "No, I'm busy." I don't prioritize my work like he does. It's my conditioning. I'm not supposed to have boundaries as a mom, society says. My work doesn't make money right now, so it's not as important as his. These are the beliefs that keep me from guarding my sacred space and creative time. I know these thoughts are not really true. I know it is good for me to have space and fulfill my needs. But, even knowing that, I don't set stronger boundaries.

Here I am complaining the week before Thanksgiving. I have so much to be grateful for, of course. We have a warm new home, the ability to live in a beautiful mountain town, pretty good health for my whole family, electricity, heaters, boots, gloves, steamy showers. The list goes on. I am obscenely privileged in some ways. I have white skin. I have a college education. I have part-time daycare for my kid even though I'm not employed. I have a kind and caring husband. I have grandparents close by that help with childcare. I have all the food I'll ever need. I am able to use my spare time to write these silly things and care for my mental health instead of working a passionless job for a meager wage. I have an able body and good looks. I have a car that I can take out to nature. I have pens and paper, a computer. Yet with all this and more, I still find myself unsatisfied.

Maybe it's me. Maybe I'll just always be unhappy. Maybe it will never be enough. Or maybe there is something more inside me, begging me to pay attention. There is an artist within who won't surrender. There are books in me, demanding to be made. There is a world out there that needs my input. There are mothers somewhere that need these words to heal and find their own satisfaction.

I am made for something more than this grueling schedule, these bags under my eyes, this confining privilege. I am here to bring something into being—many things, maybe. I am here to let words dance on pages, to stir souls from stages, to commune deeply with sages.

Yes, I am a mother. Yes, I will always be a mother. Yes, I have more responsibilities than I've ever had and they are seemingly never done. But I am also a woman. I am also an artist. I am also my own person with my own needs and my own callings. They get louder the more I ignore them, push them away, don't have time for them. They get angry when I busy myself with sweeping the floor instead of picking up a pen. They are resentful of my family. They feel trapped in this role, stifled, dulled, neglected.

I don't know how to do it all—my callings and my duties. I know I have to find a way to claim my days, but the path is not clear. What is clear, though, is I want to have it all—motherhood and career, family life and social life, security and freedom. Maybe I am insatiable, or maybe if I just had more time, more space, more of something not quite known, I would be okay.

Grinding

I am clenching my teeth at night,
grinding them off.

They are worn shorter
as the years grow longer
and I'm farther from my truth.

There's something inside of me,
trying to get out.

It's the many silenced screams
and all the un-lived dreams
I'm not brave enough to shout.

sleep dep

I startled from my sleep. The dream was still around me, vague but intoxicating, pulling me back under. I heard her cry out, and my heart jumped. I sat up quickly, too quickly. My eyes were like sand bags, sand paper—dry, gritty, heavy. I squeezed them shut and tried to open them wide. I couldn't. My vision was blurry. It was dark, but the green glow of 2:05 AM on my alarm clock illuminated my robe on the chair. I stumbled into it, covering my topless body, and shuffled on my slippers. I tipped a little, lost my balance as I walked out the door, and leaned on the frame to steady myself. She was still crying, more urgently, sobs of "Mama!"

"I'm here, I'm here," I soothed her as I opened the door. I picked her up from the crib and pulled her into the big stuffed rocking chair, cradling her on my lap, petting her head to soothe her. She nuzzled into my chest, breathing erratic.

I could feel the whispers of suicidal thoughts trying to form in my mind, like they do sometimes when I'm too sleep-deprived. I pushed them away, tried to be present. We sat and rocked, sat and rocked until her breathing became steady. Her little body twitched—hands, feet, arms. When the twitching was done, I knew she was asleep again. I placed her gently back in her crib, crept quietly out of her room, shut the door gently, and lumbered back to my room. I stripped off my robe, kicked off the slippers, groaned really loudly, rubbed my eyes, and then flopped back down in bed, flaring the covers around me dramatically. I felt like I wanted to cry, but didn't.

I tried not to think, to lull myself back to sleep, to find that interesting dream again that I couldn't quite remember but still felt. But, despite all my efforts, a Disney song implanted itself in my mind and played on repeat. I tried to shut it up, to find the quiet of sleep, to at least think a different song. But no, the same line, over and over and over and over and over and over. The whispers of death got a bit louder, trying to be heard above the song. I let out a frustrated "Argh!" and turned over in bed, shoving a pillow between my knees, curling around it.

Sometimes my husband gets up with her at night. We take turns, usually. But this week he has more work than normal, is launching a new program for his clients, and needs to be fully rested in order to work and make money for our family. So I'm the one that's been getting up with her all week. She went through a long phase earlier this year of sleeping through the night most nights. It was heavenly. I finally had some brain cells back and could think about things. But since we moved, she's been waking up at night again, often several times. Not every night, but most. This was the third night in a row of disturbed sleep for me and I was starting to lose it.

I don't know when, but I finally drifted to sleep. I was on a cruise. There was music playing, a band. I was drinking a tropical drink with an umbrella. My ex-boyfriend from college was sitting next to me on a lounge chair. He had more muscles than I remembered, and I felt a surge of attraction. He leaned over to give me a kiss and screamed, "MAMA!"

I woke up with a start, looked at my clock. 3:30 AM. Damnit. Fuck. Shit. I stumbled into my robe again and into her room. She was crying, again. I tried to just calm her down in her crib. I placed my hand on her chest with a little shaking motion, kept my eyes mostly closed, trying desperately to stay in a sleepy state without a Disney song in my head or thoughts of death. "Shhhh, shhhh," I made the classic baby sleep noise, trying to get her to calm down. She didn't, stood up, lifted her arms to me as a sign to pick her up. I felt tears forming in my eyes. I just needed some sleep, some deep sleep, and that tropical cruise kiss would be fucking nice too. I sighed, picked her up, brought her back to the chair. I held her and rocked her and silently cried. The tears streamed down my face. I didn't sob or heave. The faucet just turned on and my mind melted out of my eyeballs. It took longer for her to go to sleep this time. I stumbled back into my room at 4:25 AM, kicked off my slippers, fell into my bed with my robe still on, and held myself as I shook. I cried and cried, letting the sounds come out in a muffled way, letting my body convulse with my arms wrapped around my shoulders and knees in a ball. I felt like I wanted to go home, though I was already home. I felt like I wanted to curl back into the womb. I felt like I wanted to be buried in soil. I felt like I wanted to die.

I sobbed and shook until I was done and then fell asleep again. This time there were no dreams. At 6:30 AM she woke up and was ready to start her day. Bags under my eyes, dread in my head, I swooped her from the crib, placed her in her highchair, gave her a morning cup of milk, and made extra strong coffee. I didn't smile at her coos. I didn't laugh at her toddles. I didn't feel much of anything. Bland, broken, just surviving, cried out, touched out, sleep-deprived.

losing it

I screamed at my kid this morning over breakfast. I've never yelled that loud at her before. I've gotten mad, sure. I've lost my temper. But I haven't screamed at the top of my lungs. "YOU'RE DONE! YOU'RE DONE!"

My eyes bulged out of my head, my chest inflated, my already sore throat rasped a little with the strain. I stormed out of the room.

It was a fight about breakfast. Her, asking for something unhealthy, me, offering her everything else under the sun. Her, saying no in the whiniest, most terrible voice she could conjure and throwing her food on the floor. Me, trying to give her something else I thought she would like, something special of mine that I never give her. Her, throwing it on the floor.

I fucking lost it.

As soon as I woke up, I was in service. I got dressed and ready to go play in the snow that had just fallen because that's what she wanted to do. Then, change of plans on her part: she wanted juice. So I got her juice. Then she wanted eggs, so I made her eggs and made the whole family breakfast. Then she didn't want eggs anymore and started throwing them on the floor. The saga continued until I started yelling.

Usually I can keep it together well enough. Usually I can deal with the moods and changing whims of this toddler with relative grace. But not today.

The storm outside blew in a foot of white powder overnight. It's making me really anxious, on edge. Even though she slept through the night, I am still worn out from a week of shitty sleep. I also have a cold, so the weather is extra abrasive and I just want to rest and drink soup and tea. I want someone to take care of ME. I want to be stroked, cuddled, coddled. I want to be looked after and left alone. I don't have the energy to fight with a two-year-old. I don't have the resource to keep caretaking when I'm the one that needs support. But I have to. I'm the mom. I have to keep going, keep cooking and cleaning and keep the show running but I just want to stop and sleep, to relax and rest deep, to dream, to play, to be off for a day so I can come down from boiling back to a simmer, so I can have a glimmer of my life as my own, so I can set down the plates and just feast without having to keep them spinning in the air or cleaning them.

I am running on low to empty. I don't have enough strength left to handle all of this, to be calm through her moods, to take her abuse. So today I snapped. I cracked. I lost it.

as a mother

As a mother, I am both the softest and harshest place my daughter knows.

I can be exquisitely attuned, gentle, calming, safe—and I can be angry, loud, hostile.

I can swoop her in my arms and make everything okay as I drop into a sensitive space, enveloping her in nurturing grace, and I can explode from frustration and anxiety, raining down intensity upon her toddler protests.

Sometimes I feel bad about this. What kind of message is this sending to her? What kind of reality am I shaping where the person in her life who is the most comforting is also the most abrasive? I shame myself for my full spectrum, thinking I should be always soft, always nurture, always be sensitive and caring. That I should be able to push all my feelings aside and endlessly provide for her needs. That's what a mother is after all, isn't it? That's what I've been told.

Then I think of Mother Earth and know I am like her. She is the softest grassy meadow and a deafening hail storm. She is a tree covered in moss and lightning that sets the forest aflame. She is the beauty of a rainbow and the destruction of an earthquake. She is the tickling of a gentle breeze and a tornado that tears down houses and kills.

I am not physically abusive. I do my best to not be harmful in my harshness. Yet I can only control so much. I too am a force of nature, both beautiful and extreme. I am the daughter of the earth who both nurtures and destroys. I do my best to provide for my child with the abundance I reap, yet I cannot help the intensity of my storms. I want to protect her and keep her safe but I also am a beast that cannot help but stampede in fury when the pressure gets too high. I shelter her as best I can with my caves and branches, but I also cannot suppress the wildness of my humanity. I am only being the way the Great Mother has made me, the way this world has shaped me. If the earth is like this, both nurturing and hardening, why should I be any other way?

about me

I don't want to write about how hard it is, but it is hard. I don't want to live my life from the lens of complaining, but raising a toddler is wearing me down.

Last night after I finally got her to bed, I collapsed in a pile of tears and panic. Anxiety had welled in my belly more and more all day, gripping my gut, shortening my breath, capturing all my energy in a cage just under my ribs.

We had a pretty good morning, actually. Her daycare was closed and my husband was working, so it was a mommy-and-baby day. We went to this cool indoor trampoline park, had lunch out, she went down for her nap with relative ease. But the evening was a shit-show of tantrum after tantrum, and it took all my strength not to yell back at her. Every task invoked a screaming protest from her—dinner time, finishing dinner, taking a bath, getting out of the bath, brushing her teeth, being done brushing her teeth, reading books before bed, getting into bed. My poor nervous system was getting blasted repeatedly by someone else's frustration. I felt like a bad mom. I felt like it was my fault. I felt like if only this or that, it would be better. If only I was more emotionally available during my postpartum fiasco. If only I was more patient. If only I had read more books on how to handle tantrums. If only this whole thing was different, I was different, she was different, it all was different—then I would be a better mom and she wouldn't be so hard for me to handle.

———

Today while she was at school for a few hours, I went to a pole dancing class and swung around. I stared at my body in the mirror, grinding and doing sultry moves. My mind was totally focused on the task of learning this foreign dance form, not thinking about mothering at all. It was heavenly, like a mini-vacation. I wanted to stay in that sweaty studio forever. But eventually, I had to leave, got something to eat quickly before I picked her up, brought her home, wrestled her down for a nap, and here I am now, writing in the kitchen, drinking cold coffee hurriedly before she wakes up. A dread clouds around me, my stomach twisted in a knot of not enough time.

I know it will end eventually. She will grow up and move out and be her own person and I will get my life back, some day. But, for now, I am stuck in this endless cycle of routine.

I've never liked kids. I think they are noisy and sticky and annoying with too many needs. I always did my best to avoid them. Now, I have one. I'm around her nearly all the time and a big part of me hates it. I love her too, of course, more than I ever knew possible. I think she is the sweetest, most precious thing in the world. Even kids that aren't mine are growing on me.

But I like quiet. I like big, long books. I like serene nature with no one else around. I like loud music with heavy bass. I like nightclubs with good DJs and sexy dancing. I like weed and psychedelics. I like days and days of nothing to do besides whatever I want. I like creating art that takes time and focus. I like gathering in groups of adults and being in sacred ritual, making music, expressing ourselves fully. I like cuddle puddles. I like loud parties that go all night. I like living alone. I like being alone. I like adult humor. I like sex—frequent and soul-quenching sex. Morning sex. Loud and kinky, groaning sex. Middle-of-the-house, toe-curling sex. Then quiet that stretches on for days.

I have found ways to squeeze in a tiny bit of that within my endless routine and responsibilities of motherhood. But not enough. Not enough to be satisfied. Not enough to feel calm and fully in my body all the time. Not enough to feel self-realized, like I'm living my purpose, like I'm truly happy and fulfilled.

———

When I think about the long road ahead—about how she is only two and has so many years of needs from me to go—a hopelessness settles in. Sometimes it's a subtle despair, sometimes it's a soul-sucking depression. Sometimes it's an insane amount of anxiety that completely takes me over and I need a serious break from my regular life to pull myself out of it. How can I keep doing this for years and years? Where am I in all of this and how do I stay connected to her and myself at the same time? How do I show up for her every single day and not lose myself?

Some days, even when I've had a little break, I can't just jump into my creativity or what truly nourishes me. My mind is melted from toddler-land and I just stare into space taking deep breaths or distract myself by watching a show. Time does not equal productivity—not when I am being zapped and taken out of my flow constantly by having to serve someone else's needs or clean the house again. Satisfying creative expression is far away and inaccessible those days.

———

But then there are other days, like today, where I have a long enough break, and I do something that brings me back to my essence, like pole dancing or a long walk in nature, and I have time to sit and think while she naps and I write.

The muse is here, finally. The creative spark that I so crave has found me once again and, united, we pour words out on a page. Even in the confines of this parental prison, despite the days and days spent seemingly wasted playing with baby toys and cleaning them up, wrestling with a tantruming toddler and scraping meals off the floor, crying with my back against the closet after I finally get her to bed because I'm so exhausted and unhappy and wish I could run away but I can't and so I stay and have a meltdown because there is nothing else to do—I can still find the magic of inspiration sometimes.

———

Why did I choose this? After all, I'm pro-choice. I could have had an abortion and gotten the hell out of dodge. But I didn't. I went through with it, and I've been going through it ever since.

Somehow I didn't really think about what was in store for me. I was pregnant, I was going to have a baby. I could conceptualize that far. But my mind did not grasp that the baby would keep growing, and have more complex needs, and turn into a toddler, and have opinions that conflict with mine, and keep going and growing on and on for years...for decades, really. Now here I am, only two years in, and a huge part of me wants out.

I want my freedom back. I want my solitude. I want time with my creative process. I want romantic nights and days spent in bed. I want to just drink coffee and eat take-out and not have to clean up after anyone. I want to leave my house a mess and not care because I'm out with friends and none of it matters. I want to have the life I once had, where I would go dancing three nights in a row and attend the most epic parties that last a whole weekend and binge on psychedelics and not have to wake up at six AM on Monday morning to take care of a kid.

I want to just be my old self again and not give a fuck. But I can't.

Someone once reminded me that I very well could do whatever I want and just leave all my motherhood responsibilities behind. They reminded me that I am actually choosing to stay and be a good mom. It's my choice. I'm not trapped. I could leave. Plenty of moms leave their families. But I won't. I made the decision to be a parent and so I will stay for this kid.

This kid. This exceptional kid. Besides all her tantrums

and needs, she is quite amazing. She sings so many songs and dances and acts out dialogue from musicals and plays drums and piano and guitar. She's a pretty good mom to her baby doll, is really friendly and quite sweet when she wants to be. She loves jumping and shaking her head so her hair flies around her face and climbing on couches and lava rocks or anything else she can. She's pretty cool.

I'm not saying I don't love her. I have loved and protected her every second since she was born. But I don't like being a mom all the time. Those two things can co-exist. They do, and the distance between them is pulling me apart at the seams.

So I do things like take pole dance classes and write poems and songs in my spare time when I can muster the mind for it. I go out by myself some nights to this dirty basement bar downtown and dance wildly to electronic music, then come home quietly and crawl into bed. My husband and I go dancing every Tuesday night at an event called Ecstatic Dance where we connect with our new community and have three hours to taste freedom while my parents feed our daughter pizza and put her to bed. We get a night to ourselves here and there when the baby sleeps at her grandparents' house, but we are often so exhausted that nothing exciting happens and we go to bed early.

I have tried to create a fulfilling life within the confines of motherhood since the beginning. I've tried to make space for my creativity within it all, but nothing has quite worked out.

Now that she is finally in daycare, I am starting to get glimmers of hope. I still struggle, but I am finding bits and pieces of answers, a few at a time. This new environment, with all the snow and unfamiliar people, with all the tall trees and promises of a new beginning, has given me the opportunity to reinvent myself, to recreate myself, to remember myself and to recommit to living my truth, despite and because of all the challenges. I am dedicated and determined to have a life that I love, baby and all, and a big part of that is carving out more time for my art. In order to be happy in this life that I've haphazardly chosen, I have to prioritize this typing, this thinking, these words. I have to keep writing this into a book, for my own sanity. Having that as a goal keeps me going, keeps me alive inside. I will keep doing it. I will dedicate my mind to this task and summon the creative strength to make it happen. I must.

mother of eve

I was two months postpartum. The depression hadn't set in fully yet, but the drudgery was there. I was in my parent's big empty house alone with the baby. I sat on the floor in the open concept living room—a room no one ever used. The stuffy sofa stared back at me with starchy fabric, an ugly pattern. It was not suitable for sitting...not for me. The baby was lying next to me on a purple blanket stretched out on the carpet.

I turned my head and gazed at the dusty piano in the corner, wondering if I'd ever make music again. The baby cooed. I looked down at her, put my hand on her chest, and wiggled her a bit. She burped. I sighed. I held up a toy and shook it over her head. She smiled, I think. Hard to tell at that age sometimes.

My insides were itching. I needed to do something, something else. My brain felt dull and flat. The days were getting boring. I couldn't muster the mind for much of anything, not even reading, which I've always loved.

I watched the dust float in the light streaming in from

the window. A few minutes later she started fussing, then crying. I whipped out my boob and fed her, absent-minded, still watching the dust.

I switched boobs, finished the feeding, rocked her to sleep in my arms, laid her down, and looked around.

I felt the sudden need to write. I crept upstairs, got my computer, and came back down. It had been unused for a while. I wiped some dust off the top and opened it, placed it on the glass coffee table next to my sleeping babe, and sat on a pillow. I opened an empty document and without thinking I let my fingers dance across the keys.

Fiction came out. A made-up mythology of a goddess and lineage and mothers and daughters. Of ancestors from beyond and a creation story. When I was done, an hour had passed. At the top I wrote a title, "Mother of Eve."

The baby stirred. I closed my laptop, feeling 10 years younger. The furrow in my brow had unfolded. My eyes were relaxed. My lips—almost a smile.

I was writing again. I was doing something. I wasn't just a baby tender. I was an artist. The muse was with me and I was having thoughts and doing things besides diaper changes and staring into nothingness. I sang to the baby and took her outside. I sat by the koi pond with her in my lap and smiled at the fish. When my husband got home from work he said, "you look happy!" For that day, at that moment, I truly was.

part 4

THE CHANGING

the gifts of snow

I drove out into the glowing white abyss, the first sunny day after the storm. I was a little scared to be driving, but the streets were plowed. I was starting to get the hang of maneuvering a car on icy roads without intense fear gripping my belly.

I was suited up in my long puffy brown jacket and fleece-lined leggings, long sweater, hat, big boots, gloves in my pocket. I was still grappling with the fact that twenry-five degrees is an acceptable temperature to go outside, but got as prepared as I could.

People were everywhere, going about their shopping and outdoor adventures on this long Thanksgiving holiday weekend. I relaxed a bit and started looking around as I cruised through my new hometown. We've been here for almost a month. Time is moving fast and slow. I feel like both a tourist and a local.

Snow-covered trees snapped me into awareness of the beauty of winter. The blue sky against everything white was startling and humbling. Then, I saw them. The

Cascade Mountains. They were perfectly covered in snow, gleaming in the sunlight, completely visible and clear. My breath caught in my throat, my eyes welled up, tears fell, and I laughed out loud by myself in my car. Not a polite chuckle—a cackling, loud, insane person type of laugh that rippled out of me uncontrollably. The beauty, the majestic beauty! It was almost too much to bear.

When I got to the river, it was hard to take it all in. The snow, the big trees, the rushing water, the glimmering snow everywhere reflecting the sun. I had to be so present while walking down the trail so I wouldn't slip, abs engaged, steps intentional. The beauty and the focus brought me into an altered state of meditative trance. My thoughts were slow, my heart was full, my mind was blown into a state of quiet serenity. I was finally able to receive the gifts of the winter. I felt welcomed by this strange new world. In that moment I knew in my bones— I belong here. I am home.

stay, write, smile

I am cycling between feeling an intense urge to run away from my family, finding solace in making art out of my situation, and gushing with love and adoration for my child.

I have been gifted most of this day and night to be alone at home. I am in a state of calm focus right now. I finally have some space and time away from the daily grind to open into my creative mind and express more complex layers of my thoughts, I arrange them on a page in a way that seems like some kind of artistic contribution to mankind, however small or perhaps insignificant.

When I am making art, my life has meaning and my mind has freedom. It makes me feel like I can keep going another day and week and month and year after year after year of this domestic duty. I have to make art out of my situation in order to fully engage with it, to be more alive, to find myself, to understand my feelings, to feel significance in an otherwise insignificant seeming full-time job that never ends.

I don't have the bandwidth to create anything outside of my experience right now. I have to take the trials of my current situation and weave them into something beautiful, because that is all I have the capacity for. This is all I have to work with. My mind won't reach farther in the past and tell long-lost stories, or dive into unknown worlds to sculpt fiction, or tell tales of people and cultures far away from my own. I don't have the mental space, I don't have the time for such depth. It's all just here and now and so I am carving my little life into something creative, something interesting, something meaningful. It's all I can do.

When I am not writing, I waver between wanting to bolt and wanting my child to stay this small and sweet-smelling forever. I absolutely love my daughter and am borderline obsessed with her, but mothering without creative expression drives me crazy. So I try to keep my muse alive while caring for her—finding presence in my steps and breaths, dancing while pushing her on the swing, writing poetry in my head as I rock her to bed, listening to an inspiring audiobook in my headphones while we go on a very slow walk together. I find outlets to express myself in small ways, even just doodling or having a conversation with a stranger. But once in a while, all the tasks and duties pile up too high, crowding out the creativity until I can't hear its whispers anymore. When that happens, I want to run so far away that all I hear is river water, all I see are trees.

And then sometimes I hold her at bedtime, smell her head, and am filled with ecstasy. I feel her little hand on my arm and my heart swells. She nestles into my chest for comfort and the oxytocin explodes in my brain like fireworks. My pupils dilate, my breath deepens, my mind stills, and I relax into maternal bliss. Then a tantrum comes the next day and I forget all about it.

The only way I have found solace in this endless caretaking routine and not actually run away is to write, to write, to write this. These words are saving me, line by line. This work is keeping me sane, keeping me happy, keeping me calm, keeping me from losing it.

I am learning how to carve out more time for myself, to train my brain to find this artist space more easily, more often, to stay in the flow of inspiration even when my mind is numb from baby songs. It's not the greatest thing ever written, but it's beautiful in its own way. It's not the sprawling fantasy novel I want to write someday, but it's enough to feed my soul and quench my unending thirst for depth and beauty-making. It probably won't ever be a New York Times Best Seller, but it is keeping me from leaving my family, from hurting myself, from hating my life.

Writing this story—making art out of my little existence—is keeping me connected to something greater—to meaning and purpose, to passion and powerful surges of aliveness. So, whatever comes of this, it's worth more than gold. Whenever I forget, I remind myself—stay, honey. Stay and write. And then, I am able to smile.

untold

I aim to be vulnerable and truthful. I long to spill my guts and have it be useful. I do what I can, but it's not the whole story. There are worlds within worlds of this one life of mine. I can't say everything, I don't have the time.

I haven't shared about the people I am meeting, the dance floors I am getting down on, the friendships I am forging, the events we are planning. I haven't shared about all the endless nature walks I've taken and the beauty I'm taking in. I haven't told you about the temperature of the river water when I dip my hands in and splash my face: shockingly cold. I haven't described the fresh smell of the pines and junipers and the feel of the winter wind. I haven't written about the friends I've kept for seven years that now live all over the world, and the Zoom calls we have regularly. I haven't mentioned the way their love warms my heart and keeps me glowing even when I've convinced myself I'm all alone.

I haven't told you what it's like when I meditate, or

THE ME IN MOTHERHOOD

when I don't. I haven't spoken about my relapse, and the way I smoke weed every day now. I've kept quiet about my relationship with my husband—our sex life and what he's like. I haven't even told you his name or what he does for work, why he's absent so much of the time. I haven't told you that I'm Greek and my dad has a thick accent, that my parents and my brother are opening a restaurant here together and I'm proud of them. I haven't mentioned my brother's girlfriend and how much I love her. I haven't told you how she helps out with our daughter sometimes on Saturdays without asking anything in return. How she along with my parents have become our small but growing village.

Did you know I'm bisexual? I love women too. Did I mention that my husband and I are talking about opening up our relationship? I'm terrified and excited.

I try to be completely honest, but I haven't been because I've withheld all these truths. Yet if I told these stories, a different book would form. It wouldn't be about the Me in Motherhood. It would be about the other people in my life. It would be about addiction and relapse. It would be about the Woman in Wife. It would be something else entirely.

So, although I am as transparent as I can be, there are so many parts of me you will not see, at least not in this book. I will show you my guts and my insides, my innermost thoughts, my fears and feelings about motherhood and finding myself again. These things are the truth. But the full story is not here and never will be. There are too many moments to capture, too much nuance to mention, too many trails of tales untold. That's the way all stories go. There is so much you will never know.

Layers

I can't bear
To bare my soul
But I can't bear
Not to

I don't want to be
Totally naked
But I can't stand
All these clothes

I want to take off
All the layers
And show you
Who I am

But it's so complicated
With scarves and hats
And a lifetime of
Scars

I don't want to
Be alone in here
Under all these
Layers

But the thought
Of showing you
Everything I am
Is terrifying

So I will just
Unveil one piece
At a time
Slowly

And eventually
You will see
Most of
What I mean

It won't be
The same
As being
Totally bare

But at least
I won't be
So stuffy
And alone

my morning

I am sitting here, drinking coffee and writing poetry because that's what gives me pleasure. I'm at a restaurant and it's starting to fill up. I come here once a week. It's the best place in town and I could smell the muffins and coffee wafting from inside as I walked up the icy path.

I'm sitting here, taking up the corner table by the window, computer out, headphones on, purple hat accidentally matching my purple pants. I take sips of my warm, dark drink with coconut milk, waiting for my food.

I just placed my order. I like to wait a while to order, giving myself a chance to drink coffee and write something meaningful. This place really is the very best in town and it's a privilege to get to sit here for so long. In about twenty minutes, the restaurant will be full and I will feel that familiar pressure of the nice waitstaff, not asking me to leave but gently guiding me along the dining process so I will exit in a timely manner and make space for the chilly people waiting at the door, ready for their coffee and

THE ME IN MOTHERHOOD

breakfast.

I come here once a week. I get here early, before the crowd, after I drop my daughter off at school. I call it school but it's really daycare at someone's home. It's just down the street from this restaurant and across the way is one of my favorite nature parks.

After I drink a lot of coffee and eat a little breakfast, I take the rest to go, place the container on the floor of my little Prius, and head over to the nature preserve that runs along the river. It's a pristine place with a perfect bridge leading to a large expanse of gently tamed wilderness, full of junipers and pines and huge lava boulders, more magnificent than most rocks I've seen. It startles me into presence every time, having such beauty and openness so close. All I have to do is drive up and walk across the bridge and it's there, waiting for me every time, sparkling fresh. I feel beckoned to commune with the vastness and the pretty pines, to sink into their wisdom, leaning against their strong trunks as I watch the water go by. Often there is barely another person in sight and I find myself alone with nature, alone with my thoughts, alone with the great unknown and the power of creation.

Then I run errands, my morning of majestic grace complete, my escape from the cycle of the mundane over. I pick up my daughter at noon and wrestle her down for a nap. Once she is asleep, which often takes a while, I clean the house or call a friend, bake some bread or make lunch for me and my husband. The time she is sleeping quickly goes by and then it's afternoon playtime. I drag myself into a happy face and find ways to engage with my growing, rambunctious, opinionated, beautiful, annoying, wonderful two-year-old.

But for now, I'm sitting here drinking my coffee and writing some words that bring a touch of meaning to my reality. This time, this ritual—writing and drinking and eating and looking out the window and taking too much time at a busy restaurant but leaving a large tip so I don't feel so bad about it—this is my sanctuary. This is my respite in the middle of it all. These words, this black mug full of steamy liquid, this food that was just delivered, so fragrant and fluffy—the best muffin in the world and some eggs and things—these are my vacation within the incessant demands of my life. This is one place where I create my art. This is a moment with the infinite.

The restaurant is quickly filling up. I will eat my fill, surrender my table to someone else, and get on with my day.

writer's frost

I have thought of so many things to write and then deleted them in my head. As I sit to type now, I feel some fear. What if I don't do it right? What is the best thing to share and say?

Each of us is such a complex puzzle. We are made up of pain and pleasures, perceptions and moods. We are a combination of everything that's happened, mixed with our genes mixed with our fears and our mother's fears and our grandmother's traumatic childbirths because the DNA remembers and passes it down. It's all jumbled together inside us, causing us to be how we are, see how we see, feel how we feel, and choose what we choose.

Most of the time, I am a riddle even to myself. The thing that is "me" is ever-changing. I have many sides, many ways of seeing things, many ways of being—as do you.

One side of me is scared right now. She is afraid this isn't any good. She is afraid that her writing will never amount to anything and this is a huge waste of time—a futile exercise of typing with semi-cold fingers in a parked car facing a wooded river at dusk.

The car is not on and therefore the heat is not either and my toes are still stinging with frostiness from my walk in the forest by the glassy water. There is snow on the ground and, as I walked through the deeper parts, the tips of my boots got covered and cold.

When I got down to the trail from the parking lot, the crunch crunch of white was so satisfying. Then, in the melted parts, the exquisite softness of the earth beneath my soles sent electric waves of enjoyment through my whole body, lighting me up with a buzzing aliveness. I paused to take it in, marveling at the ground below me. When I looked up, the trees became more pronounced and the sea of green overwhelmed me with rippling beauty that pulsated my eyesight, vision expanding to take it all in.

It has taken a long journey to be able to experience nature like this. I have sharpened my senses with embodiment work, trauma healing, psychedelics...plus the marijuana I ingested when I got here. It's not just the weed, though. There are things in my past that have shaped me into a sensational and sensitive being, capable of seeing and feeling things others often do not. When I am present enough, I can perceive an aliveness in the world that is beyond the ordinary. I will try to tell you about it with the words I write, but it will never be the full picture.

As I face my fears about writing this book, I find a deeper truth. I've discovered that in order to move forward, I have to accept that storytelling requires letting go. Whatever is written will have to be good enough. These words that I choose to take down—and not the ones I don't—will be the way this tale moves forward. The color I cast on the telling of my life will vary on the day and the mood and the amount of patience I have. There are millions of experiences and feelings that will not make the cut. Only these ones, these little black words on this stark white page, will tell the story. I have to accept this and let go of perfectionism. I have to believe that the muse within me and my own abilities will carry us forward across the page into something coherent and beautiful.

I will trust the power of my words, the wisdom of my choices. I will let go of the fear of doing it wrong or badly and be with the momentum of the moment. I will surrender to this calling, this feeling, this rightness of writing. I will let it heal me from the inside out and pray for the courage to share it one day. I will let these sentences form flames of love around me, melting my writer's frost, so the book can go on.

the best things are

I crave the deafening silence of the deep forest and I am also scared of it.

I don't like being lonely, but I love to be alone. I push away everyone I love at some point, but it is always when I want them closer. I can't stand crowds but long to be lost in the waves of a city. I want to be closer to my daughter but also need more space.

My nervous system is tricky. I run on high anxiety. I don't know if this is a result of becoming a mother or if I have always been this way but didn't quite notice.

I feel good a lot of the time lately, too. I feel pleasure. I can even relax sometimes and not be anxious. But in general, it's there and something I deal with daily.

Sometimes I question my parenting choices and wonder if it would all be easier if I had done things differently. When she acts out, my mom brain immediately thinks it must be my fault. If only I had done this or that, she wouldn't be like this, and maybe I would be different too. Maybe I wouldn't have so much anxiety if

I was more bonded to her. Maybe she would have fewer tantrums if I was more available.

———

Today I met with a mom of another two-year-old who still breastfeeds and co-sleeps and hasn't spent more than four hours away from her kid, ever. I envied her a little. I don't actually wish that was my reality, but I wish that I had the capacity to tolerate being so connected with my child without feeling like I'm going to die or run away or kill myself.

What the heck happened to me that I'm so unable to be this interwoven with another being? I demand independence. Am I naturally an introvert and need space, or am I deeply traumatized from something I can't quite remember? Maybe I never experienced true nervous-system regulation and bonding with my own parents and I had to develop a strategy of self-sufficiency in order to survive as a small child. Is it my nature, or because of my nurturing?

I don't know what the source is or if it's healthy or sad. I don't know if it's extremely damaging to my child that I'm like this or not that bad. Is it better to be hyper-connected to our parents or to have more spaciousness and freedom? The verdict is out. If I compare our two toddlers, it appears that mine is actually more well-adjusted. She is more consistently cheerful, though she does have tantrums. She is nicer to other kids, though she did go through a pushing phase around one year old. She is loving to her parents and other family members. The other kid is moody and mean, both to other children and to his father, who he kicks in the balls regularly. Is it nature or nurture that has grown them this way? Is my more spacious parenting style actually beneficial for my daughter's growth, or was she just born with a friendlier disposition? Is the other boy's constant connection with his mother actually damaging to his development, or is this just his personality? I don't know.

———

What I do know is that since my daughter has been in daycare for over a month now, I am feeling a lot better. It has afforded me time to do what gives me fulfillment. I have more creative clarity than I've had in a long time, and more happiness.

After two years of confusion caused by my unexpected mother role, I have finally found my way back to my own desires. If I was deep in the throes of attachment parenting, I wouldn't have these little bursts of time for myself and the growing joy that comes with it.

I'm still anxious, but it's less consuming than before. I'm sure depression and overwhelm will return, but I can't imagine they will carry me so far away from myself again. There is a new level of grounding that has entered my being by choosing this way, this space, this time. Though, now that I am actively working towards my goal of writing this book, and starting to dream into what business I will create for myself, I do notice some fear comes up.

I crave a life of powerful purpose and I'm also scared of it. I want to share my art far and wide but I'm afraid no one will want to hear it or I'll fail somehow and slide back down to a meaningless existence of washing dishes and doing laundry forever. I long to taste the freedom of making my own money again, to have a business that makes an impact, but I'm terrified I will burn out. I want so badly for my dreams to come true that I'm scared they never will.

Even with all this going on, I am committed to keep typing, keep feeling, keep learning, keep sharing, keep dreaming, keep believing in myself, keep finding time for me within all this mothering. I have to keep going or I will surely wither away. It is both enlivening and utterly terrifying—just like all the best things are.

Vulnerable?

If I
Let myself be seen
And meet rejection
Or am ignored
Will I be okay,
Or will I crumble?

Is my true face
A fragile pile of rubble
Ready to dismantle
At a quake
Of dismissal—

Or am I a mountain range
Made of volcanos
Exploding thousands of times
Over millions of years
And the crumbling is just
A part of the growth?

women's night

We gathered like a small coven, mugs of hot tea in hand, sitting on the floor, propped up by pillows under our butts. Candles glowed and soft light illuminated our eager faces. The living room smelled of spice and flowers, incense burning somewhere in the background.

We sat in a circle and, one by one, we shared our stories. We revealed our hardships and told of our glories. We took turns in an orderly way that came naturally, shifting to each woman in time with our full attention. We were vulnerable. We were truthful. We were together in a real way.

After everyone had a chance to share in-depth, the conversation flowed in a more informal way. At one point I let myself be quiet and listen, the chatter and laughter of female voices washing over me in a euphoric symphony. This was real friendship. This was real connection. I felt joy spiral through me and pool between my eyebrows in an intoxicating moment of delight. My eyes fluttered. My lips quivered with pleasure.

I was the only mother in the group. It didn't matter. The bond of female friendship was thick and welcoming. We stayed there late into the evening, candles burning low, teacups filled and emptied several times. When it was finally time to leave, we all stood up and hugged. I breathed in the scent of essential oils and shampoo. I basked in the soft fleshiness of each embrace. I smiled a toothy smile and let myself take it all in.

Before I drove away, I sat in my car and cried happy tears. They seeped gently from my eyes in sweet relief. My heart was full, my head was empty. I finally have a real group of friends for the first time in years. I belong.

celebrating

I got on a Zoom call with my old friends. We all used to live in Berkeley together. Our lives were interwoven back then, full of cuddles, sleepovers, random hangouts, neighborhood walks, dance parties, knocks on the door asking, "Hey, what are you up to?" that led to dinners and days spent together, existing. Eventually we all moved to different places but have kept in touch with our monthly video calls and the ever-active text stream.

"You guys!" I gushed when we were all present. "I have real friends here!"

They responded with authentic enthusiasm. Someone clapped with glee.

One of the main topics I've shared with this group over the past years has been my deep loneliness. If not for their consistent love from afar, I would have felt like I had no one. Through our many years together in Berkeley, I learned what real community was. I learned what it meant to truly belong, to be loved despite my flaws, to be vulnerable, to be supported. I've been longing for that feeling again—that depth of friendship—ever since I left five years ago.

Having my need for connection met is one of the biggest contributors to my happiness. Now that I am feeling a sense of belonging and friendship here in Bend, my life is changing. Combined with a little more time to myself because my daughter is in daycare, and the deepening purpose I feel from committing to write this book, I feel myself being remade on the inside.

I'm less grumpy. I'm less sad. I'm less anxious. I'm less frustrated with my husband. I'm less apathetic. I'm more cheerful. I have more joy, more calm, more inner peace, more patience. I'm becoming a version of myself in motherhood that I have previously only dreamed of. I am turning into a person that always seemed out of reach to me.

I thought I would perpetually feel trapped in this mom role. But I am learning how to grow myself within it, how to water my needs and feed my desires so that I blossom in this garden. The fence of restrictions and responsibilities used to feel like a cage. Now, it's a trellis that I get to lean on for stability and wind around in a way that supports my fruiting.

I am beginning to have the depth of friendship and abundance of community I've craved for years. I am learning to make more time for my creative expression. I am letting myself have that time by having more childcare help. I am beginning to actually enjoy it all and let go of the eons of obligation and guilt I've held in my cells and perceptions. I am learning to get my needs met so I can be happy in this motherhood role. After sharing all this with my dearest friends on the call, we celebrated.

my birthday

I emerged from the rose-scented bathtub. Steam rose off my body. The candlelight illuminated my curves in a luscious, romantic way and I paused to admire myself. I dried off gently, taking my time. I leisurely walked to my daughter's empty room in the quiet, still house. It was a sunny morning and that was the only place where the light streamed in the windows. I laid down and let the sunlight caress my body, indulging in the sensuality of the experience. Once I was dry, I picked up a bottle of sesame oil and slowly lubed up my whole body while the sunlight made horizontal stripes on me through the blinds. I gazed at my voluptuous form and reflected. It was the day of my birth and this was exactly how I wanted to spend it.

This body birthed a baby. This body gained seventy pounds in the process. This body lost sixty of it, and is beginning to look like "me" again. This thirty-three-year-old form has lived so many experiences, survived so many hardships, dreamed so many dreams. Its breasts are a bit saggier and more rippled than before. Its belly is flabbier and sticks out a little. Its thighs have grown in size but also in muscle.

This body was a home to another human for over nine months. This body created life. This body has held my soul through the dark nights and strange trips, carrying me into my empowerment. This body is definitely a woman now, there is no question anymore.

After I had my fill of indoor sunbathing and admiring my naked form, I got up and dressed myself for the day. I planned to go on a little hike at my favorite spot before picking up my daughter from school to meet my family for a birthday lunch. As soon as I left the house, though, the clouds came over and it started to rain. I cursed my luck, but kept on driving. I thought of turning back or doing something else, but a voice inside me urged me on. "Just go," it said. "Go to your spot." So I did.

As I got closer, a giant rainbow appeared. It graced the sky and landed right where I was driving. I followed the colors to my river-front forest walk. When I pulled up, I felt myself in conversation with the elements. The gratitude I felt for the rainbow bubbled over and I found myself asking, "Can you please stall the rain a little bit, so I can have a nice walk here before lunch?"

"Sure!" the sky replied. I giggled because I knew it really was listening and responding to me. As I got out of my car, the sun started peeking through the clouds and the rain let up. I began my walk across the bridge to the trail and it turned into the lightest drizzle, barely a rain at all. I felt elated and ran across the bridge, up the trail, and down the path. The atmosphere was giving me gifts on the day of my birth and I was delighted.

I only had about twenty minutes before it was time to

get my kid, so I took it in as best I could, breathing deep, drinking in the landscape with my eyes, touching trees and rocks and saying thank you, filling myself with appreciation that bubbled over through my heart. As I headed back to my car, the rain picked up again, and by the time I closed my door and started the engine, it was a full-on rain once more. I thanked the weather for being so kind to me on this day. As I pulled out, I was greeted with an even brighter rainbow leading the way to my daughter's school.

We headed to lunch with my family and it was lovely. My mother gave me an heirloom bracelet from her grandmother and told us family stories I had never heard before. I cried as she spoke and took in the beauty of the experience of learning about my lineage. When we left for home, yet another rainbow stood even brighter, stronger, prouder in the sky. My day was truly graced. My heart felt buoyant and full of appreciation for all the gifts, both from humans and from the earth. I felt deeply connected to everything and spent the rest of the day doing exactly what I wanted—tea and cuddles with my husband while our child napped, playing with our daughter together in the evening. I made dinner for my family and then I went to an incredible, magical, life-changing all-women's singing circle and got high from the bliss of syncing up our voices in harmony.

It was my favorite birthday yet—simple, pleasurable, full of family and miracles. I made a wish at the end of the night that this year is the year I will fully step into my creative power beyond doubt and self-sabotage. At the end of this year, I want to look back and say that yes, this has definitely been the best year of my life.

Yes I am She

Last night I glanced in the mirror for a second
and was startled because I saw my future self.
It was me, here now, but her—
the her I've always wanted to be.

She was here in my face looking back at me
and I saw a flash of how accomplished I can be.
It's not like I was super rich or successful—
I was just fully relaxed in my own skin.

I was so calm, cool, empowered—
like my clothes fit just right and
my boots were hip yet functional,
eyes blazing with certainty.

That future me was in the right place at the right time,
fully present and alive, animated by purpose,
at one with the universe in ways I have only dabbled in
but am starting to feel more often.

That's the self I am becoming,
the truest thing I know my soul to be.
And in fact she is already here
because I saw her in the mirror last night—

Looking right back at me.

idea mode

I sat in the coffee shop, gnawing on my pen. I stared at the white screen, cursor blinking. I looked over at my notepad. Scribbles and scrawls of ideas were everywhere. I want to start a business again. I want financial freedom again. I'm tired of being dependent on this man and doing all the housework to make up for it. I'm tired of not being able to leave and go on a weekend trip because he says we can't afford it. I'm tired of wearing hand-me-down clothes and Goodwill scores. I am going to make my own money. It's time.

I used to do it so easily. I would have an idea, make a website, tell some people about it, make a post, and then clients would jump into my basket. I would meet people out in the real world that had a problem I could help fix and invite them into a healing or coaching session. Then they would pay me several hundred or sometimes thousands of dollars to work with me. I felt fulfilled, on purpose. My work flowed with ease. I didn't have to try that hard to find clients. A lot of the time it just happened.

But I didn't have a kid. I didn't have endless household responsibilities. I didn't have a full-time job of homemaker in addition to the healing or coaching work. When I was done with my job, I was off. Now, if I start a business, when I'm off I'm still on. There are no real days off in motherhood. Weekends are even more full of caregiving than weekdays. Afternoons are a blur of parks and toys and playing pretend, followed by making dinner, eating dinner, cleaning dinner, bath time, story time, bedtime.

I have to start small. I am just getting back to myself. I am just finding some joy again after years of strife. I am just finding the me inside who could actually be a healer or teacher of some kind again. She's been gone a long time.

I have to create something that doesn't take a lot of time or energy, something that comes natural to me, something that is fun. Maybe something to do with dancing, or creativity, or performing. Those things light me up and ooze out of me...when I'm in the right state of mind. These last few years, that's all been far away from me, but it's coming back. I've been pulling out my guitar more often, singing my old songs. I've been dancing in my bedroom at night with my headphones on, going crazy to the electronic bass music. I've been having ideas for shows and stand-up comedy routines. I even wrote a song last month and performed it for our friends one night. Maybe the performing arts is where I am most useful at this time. Maybe I can help other people open up their artistic and creative sides with all the embodiment practices and creative cultivation techniques I know.

Or maybe I should get back into healing and do some reiki sessions. Those are really relaxing and fulfilling for me. It doesn't take any mind power—I could do it even if I was sort of low energy. Maybe I could use my friend's chiropractic office to do sessions. Or I could bring some clients to our house while the baby was at school. Maybe I could teach reiki healing again, do some trainings. That could be fulfilling and bring in some cash.

Or a writing group! I could start a women's writing group, help other people write their memoirs, hold space for the deep healing process that comes from writing truth. But, if I was marketing and running a business, and taking care of my family more than full-time hours, when would I have time to work on my own book? When would I have time to take care of myself?

The balloon of excitement in my chest deflated a bit. My shoulders slumped. I looked up from my computer. A hot guy walked into the coffee shop. He was wearing a beanie and a puffer jacket, the unofficial Bend winter uniform. His eyes were bright blue and stood out sharply against all the tan and brown of the trendy coffee shop. He walked by a wall of potted plants, the green of the leaves matching his jacket. I watched him out of the corner of my eye, hoping he wouldn't notice me looking at him.

I need to have time to form new relationships, too. Not just friendships. I want another lover.

I have been realizing this more lately. My creative energy is waking up, and so is my sensuality. My husband is so busy, our relationship has gotten complicated—there is so much baggage from our past we haven't unpacked, there isn't time. We barely ever have sex anymore. I feel like my body and heart are starving. Since we got married, we have talked about the possibility of having an open relationship. But with the kid and the postpartum depression and the busyness with trying to stay afloat financially and the move...we haven't had the space or energy. It hasn't been the right time. Now, though...

I watched the man take his cup of hot coffee to a table near me. With his back to me, he pulled off his jacket, revealing a tight, black long-sleeve shirt. Under that, his muscles rippled. I licked my lips involuntarily. I shook my head, snapping out of my daze, and turned my attention back to my computer.

Multiple half-cooked ideas scrawled across the screen. Meanwhile, my book—this book—sat unaltered on the desktop, ignored for days. I re-read all the notes I wrote on business ideas while taking sips of my cold coffee. I sighed. I didn't know the right move. I didn't know how I would do any of it, anyway. I barely have time to work on this book and take care of myself. There's not really space for a business right now. But I want it. I want that empowerment, that independence, that sense of purpose so badly. And I want another relationship. And I want more time exploring my artistic self. And I want more time with friends. And I want more time in nature. And I want to finish and publish this book. And I want weekends away. I want, I want, I want...

Suddenly I felt dizzy, like my brain was going to explode. I looked at the clock on my phone. There was one hour left before I had to get my kid. I gazed at the hot guy one more time, then packed up my stuff. I had to move my body in nature before I picked her up, or else I would be an angry, anxious mess all day. With one last sigh, I put my backpack on and strolled to my car in the parking lot, turned on the engine, and left.

all the parts

My mind wants to make things happen. My anxiety wants to know what to do. My ego wants something to show for who I am. My pride wants to make things and think they reflect on me. My insecurities want me to have something to prove my worth. My hands want something to be busy with, so I don't pick the skin around my fingers while I fret. My feet want something to run towards, so I can get out of this angsty limbo.

My belly wants to relax and release this ball of tension it is holding. My eyes want to gaze without trying to see. My heart wants to unfurl and curl up with someone by a fire, content in the moment, no need to change or do or fix anything. My spirit wants to rest in calm peace, relaxing into what is. My lungs want to exhale deeply and fill with fresh air.

My wise self wants to surrender to the winter season and just be. My impatience wants everything to happen now.

And my whole body wants to sink way down and rest, rest, finally just be okay and let it all go.

burnout

It was all going great, until it wasn't anymore. I rode the high of my newfound freedom and ideas into a crash. Yesterday, instead of writing or hiking or making a business plan or doing anything productive, I laid in bed, nauseous and tired beyond reason. Coffee in the morning didn't help me wake up; it made things worse.

I wasn't ill, but I felt sick. The anxiety in my belly had built to an unbearable level and I couldn't go on. My body forced me to rest in an uncomfortable way while my daughter was at school. I tossed and turned and moaned. Finally I found one position on my side that made the discomfort subside and stayed there. If I moved, it returned, making me feel like I was going to hurl. The nausea gripped me, for no reason other than burnout.

――――

I tossed and turned in bed, my mind running away from me, making me feel even more nauseous. After a few hours of this self-inflicted torture rest, I reluctantly got out of bed and forced some toast into my body. I had no appetite, but I had to go get my daughter soon and I needed some fuel. It helped a little, but not a lot. I went to the bathroom and splashed water on my face. I stared in the mirror and was sad to see myself that way. I was no longer Her, the empowered beautiful version of myself I saw before. I was strung out. My eyes were dark, bags swollen and grey. They lacked the lustrous shine I'd seen in them the past week.

"Fuck," I said out loud, gripping the edge of the sink. "I can't do this."

I have to rest more. I can't push so hard and fast to make something of myself beyond motherhood. These four hours, four days a week are not enough to do it all. I can't make myself so busy during my time off and then launch right into mothering afterward. I can't work all morning and then work all night as a parent. I have to find a better balance. I have to scale back my ambition.

That realization made me cry. I watched myself in the mirror as my face scrunched up and turned red. Tears trickled down my face. I thought these little bits of time would be enough to do what I need to be happy—to make something to share with the world, to write this book and create a small business again, to have a life outside of motherhood. Now I see it will never be enough to truly have it all. I have to let go of those dreams again. I have to take care of myself more deeply during those hours, so I can keep showing up for my family and not burn out.

As I realized this, staring in the mirror, I felt my heart sink and stomach clench again. This is not the end of my journey to find myself in this motherhood maze. This is still very much the middle, or maybe even the beginning.

I tried to take a deep breath, but suddenly sobs wracked my chest. Another layer of grief unclenched and spilled out. I sank to the bathroom floor and curled up on the rug, shaking with tears.

After the crying subsided, I stayed there, wrapped around myself—cold linoleum on my feet, dirty bathroom rug soft on my cheek. There, I was finally able to take some deep breaths. The grief had emptied the nausea. My stomach relaxed. A wave of acceptance flowed over me. "This is not the end," I whispered. I sighed, but instead of crying again, a small smile formed on my lips. "Okay. I can do this," I said more loudly. I gently moved to my knees, then gripped the counter to help me stand. I felt dizzy but more relaxed. I looked at my face in the mirror again. It was puffy. The dark bags were still there. But there was a quietness in my eyes. I stood there for a few moments, deciphering the meaning.

I am not done with this journey and it's not a sprint. It's not even a race. If I push myself too hard, I will fall. This time to myself is a step on the path, but it's not the whole answer. I have to scale back my expectations. I have to let myself sink deeper into presence and relaxation in my time off, not put pressure on myself to produce something.

Someday I will have more time and space to devote to my art and create a business again while still being able to take care of myself and my family. I know it will happen eventually. But it's not right now. I'm still recovering from years of mothering. I'm still healing. I'm still growing into someone who can handle more than everything I already do. But it will come. That's what my calm eyes in the mirror were saying to me.

It will come in time, but I'm not there yet. I'm here. If I slow down and savor the moments instead of wishing there were more of them, if I release the pressure and relax into presence, I will be okay. I will get there eventually—to a sense of fulfillment, a balance of career and art and self and family. But now, there is simply not enough time for it all, and I have to learn to be okay with that.

I took another deep breath, splashed my face with cold water again, dried it off with a purple towel, and gently applied some moisturizing oil, eye cream, and tinted sunscreen. I took my time with it, caressing my face, mustering all the self-love and tenderness I could in that moment. "You got this," I told the tired but calm woman in the mirror. "Be patient."

purpose

O h, what I could do if I only had the time. I am so capable, so smart, so brimming with desire to serve the world. I want to use my skills and talents to make this a better place. I want to help people, change things, create stuff. I want to do something, be somebody, have a grand purpose. I want to contribute beyond the bounds of this home, beyond the confines of my parenting duties, beyond the limits of domestic life.

If I wasn't a mom, I could do so much. I could start a non-profit or a business. I could heal a lot of people with my touch and guidance. I could create communities that serve the needs of other people emotionally and spiritually. I could write tons of books and support people's imaginations to thrive.

If I just had the brain space, the blank space, the free time to think and dream and create...I could, I would.

I can't.

I don't have the time or energy.

I lust for being useful, for being impactful, for being

big and seen and helpful. But right now, I'm a mom. Right now, the greatest use of my hands and mind is to raise this child. The most important thing to do with my attention is to give it to her. I wish I could be fulfilled with that. I wish I could truly believe that giving my love and care to this girl is enough of a contribution to the world. Maybe it really is. I can't wrap my head around it.

———

Last week, we were at the market getting the groceries: apples and cheese and such. She was sitting in the little seat of the shopping cart, facing me, snug between my protective arms on the handle. I left her a few feet away for a moment, went over to grab some noodles and contemplate the sauce. I went into a sort of trance, scanning the ingredients of every jar for the least additives, the most natural stuff I could find for quick and easy dinners. I heard her laugh loudly and snapped my head towards her, suddenly back at attention.

An old lady in a motorized chair with a basket on the front had stopped next to her and they were deep in conversation. My kid was babbling something, the lady was laughing. The lady said something in reply, leaning forward, tilting her head back and forth in a playful way. My daughter erupted in shrieks and giggles. She noticed me coming towards them, her face brightening with a "Mama!"

"Who's this?" I cooed, putting a hand back on the cart, placing the noodles and sauce in the trench.

"Mama! Friend!" My daughter laughed again and looked at the lady. The lady did a round of peek-a-boo behind her hands, sending my child into an opera of giggles again. The older lady smiled hugely, her wrinkled skin creasing at the corners.

"I gotta go now." She patted my daughter's tiny hand gently. "Bye, little one." She waved. My daughter waved back, still smiling. "Thanks for playing with me today." The old woman smiled at me and winked, patted my arm. "You have a precious gem there." She turned her head back to my daughter for a moment, then looked me in the eyes. "Good job, Mama. You are raising an incredible human. I haven't laughed that much in months." She smiled again with no teeth showing, patted my arm one more time, looked off in the distance for a second, and then pushed the button to make her seat stroll forward.

"Bye bye!" My daughter waved. "Bye friend!" She turned her attention back to me with another huge grin, then clapped her hands and said, "Yay friends!"

———

Last night we were at my parents' house—husband, baby, and all. They had been watching our daughter for the last few hours and we had just arrived to pick her up. When we walked in the door, she was dressed in a princess outfit, bows in her hair. "Ready?" my mom prompted her as we rounded the corner into the living room. Our daughter gave her grandma a thumbs-up. Grandma pushed *Play*.

Our daughter twirled around and sang loudly to her favorite Disney song. Arms wide, short blond hair flying outwards as she spun—she was a vision of joy. She belted out the melody but butchered the words, which makes sense since she can't fully speak yet, just choppy partial sentences. But she hit every note, even the high ones. She smiled and frolicked around while we all watched her, showing off some choreographed dance moves, shaking her head with emotional fervor at the intense parts of the song.

When she was done, she took a bow. We were silent for a moment, then erupted in applause. My mom was beaming. I haven't seen her smile that big in a while. My dad was grinning goofily, clicking off his phone camera after recording the whole ordeal. My daughter ran up and hugged our legs.

"Wow," my husband mused, absorbing the impact of her charging embrace.

"Wow," I agreed, nodding in amazement.

———

My daughter is a gift to this world. She brings smiles and joy to those around her. She lights up the days of strangers. She brings incomprehensible happiness to her grandparents and other family members. Her life is not insignificant. It's important. It makes a difference for others. By raising her this way, by helping her to feel safe in the world, by encouraging her to be friendly and confident and artistic, I am making a difference. If only I could fully ground into the truth that putting my energy towards raising her, instead of turning it outward to the world somehow, is truly impactful and worthwhile.

I want to let go of my ambition, my outward striving for greatness, my insatiable need to do something or be someone out there. I want to turn my attention fully to my family, to find joy and fulfillment in it, to source my sense of purpose there. I've tried this before—tried to shift my priorities and be content with domestic life. It didn't work. But I'll try again.

I won't let go of making my art, of writing these words—that is too important for me to lose sight of. But I can relax around the other stuff. I can stop thinking I need to start a business or contribute something greater to humanity. I can stop stressing myself out trying to do it all right now. I can rein my energy back, ground it down in my body, and pay attention to what I am doing already.

I am contributing here and now. My life does have meaning and purpose just as it is. Maybe, if I am able to believe that for a time, I can find some peace.

leaving too soon

I love living here. I love the crisp air. I love the way the clouds layer on top of each other in beautiful patterns and colors when a storm is coming through. I love the pine trees and the junipers, the sagebrush and the big lava rocks. I love the sunny winter days when it's in the thirties but I can still get a little vitamin D on my skin by lifting my sweater to show my belly to the light. I love all the trails and paths, the forest strolls and river walks, the mountain hikes that are only a few minutes or miles away from my home. I love the way it smells and how taking a deep breath outside brings me into a state of presence and gratitude. I love the new friends we are making, the way they smile when they see us, the way their hugs feel— warm and comfortable. I love the way they reach out and invite me places, or ask to come over for a cup of tea. I love dancing with them every Tuesday night and finding our rhythms and grooves together. I love having them over to make music in our little living room, shakers and drums on beat, voices open, hearts syncing, eyes wide, sound swirling. I even love the snow, the way it caresses the landscape and clings to the trees, making everything look magical and new.

I love this place, it's true. But still, the stress is here. I carry anxiety around with me, tucked in my gut, holding it there. It hasn't fully gone away, even with all this time, friendship, and beauty. The overwhelm is still with me, lurking in the shadows. When the dishes pile up too high and the tantrums are too many and I forget to take care of myself and stop being patient with my creative and business plans...I explode. I cry. I panic. I snap. I get mean or sharp with my family. It's still here.

I have a little more space in my days so I can mostly keep it at bay. It's far enough away that I can enjoy myself sometimes, but still close enough to let me know it's there when the pressure gets too high. I wish I could have a staycation—time alone here in Bend to fully relax and replenish. How much time would be enough to actually heal? A week, a month, a year, a decade? I won't get it. I have to learn to make do with the few hours a day I get without my daughter. I have to learn to surf the stress and come back to the joy without imploding, to dance through the endless responsibilities instead of collapsing, to take care of myself deeply during that time instead of trying to work, to be okay with where I am and not wish I was further along on this path.

———

In two days, we leave on a three-week trip. It's a vacation, technically, but not the type I crave. It will be filled with my husband's extended family and not enough childcare. I will have to take on more responsibilities than I have in a while, in unfamiliar places with unknown variables. We go to Portland for a few days, then Hawaii with his dad and siblings, then down to San Diego to see more family. It will be interesting but probably even more stressful.

I don't really want to go. I like it here. Life is good. This childcare routine is helping me so much, even though it's not quite enough time to do everything I wish I could. Now that I am scaling back and slowing down, I feel more resourced. I am taking longer walks. I am singing and dancing with no agenda. I am putting my business ambition on hold for a while and taking better care of myself.

The land here is beautiful and nourishing. The pace of living is slower than I'm used to and it suits me. The roads are easier to navigate without the huge freeways that I used to drive every day. The people are kinder and gentler. The restaurants are cozier. The coffee is tastier. The pastries are fluffier. The sky is vaster. The mountains are taller. The grass is greener, so to speak.

I want to stay and sink my roots deeper and deeper into a sense of belonging I have craved for years. It's here. I can have it. It is available for me. I'm starting to experience it.

I'm ready to stay here for a long time. I am giving myself to this place and, in turn, this place is giving itself to me. It feels a bit like falling in love. It might just be the honeymoon phase, but I feel like it's real this time. The elation, the wonder, the startling presence, the discoveries, the community connections—all bring me into a state similar to the joy after a third date, when things are going really well and you just want to stay together forever and keep uncovering the beauty of each other.

I am falling in love with Bend—the people, the land, the way of life, and even my husband again in a deeper way. I can't get enough and don't really want to leave. But in a few days, we will pack enough clothes for three different climates and embark on an adventure that I don't really want but am obligated to take.

part 5

TRAVELING

bliss visits

Last night, we walked together through Portland, strolling its dirty, dim streets. A gentle rain was falling. There were barely any lights. My baby was strapped to me, secure and snug; my husband held my elbow, guiding and protecting us. Though it was dark and cold, I felt safe and happy.

Our daughter sang loudly and persistently as we made our way home from dinner. She was wearing a bright yellow rain jacket and slick purple boots that hung down by my hips. She was strapped in snugly to my front, cuddling my chest. I hugged her tightly with my arms, both of us joyful to be so close together.

We had gone out to meet my long-time friend and her husband for a rich meal of Lebanese food. They live in Portland. We chose a place that was close to our Airbnb so we could walk there. It was a sweet night of too much food and just enough adult conversation in between paying attention to the baby's antics. There was lots of laughter and tons of bread. I felt a floaty natural high as we walked back through tiny alleys and along a busy main street to our little apartment.

We are here in Portland for two nights on our way to the Big Island of Hawaii. It's just us, our little nuclear family, resting and adventuring before we meet up with my husband's dad and his two siblings in the islands.

We flew in yesterday after a two-hour delay at the airport in Bend. I am amazed by our parenting skills and how symbiotic we all are together. Our two-year-old companion didn't have one meltdown during the five hours of travel. She passed out in the Uber ride from the airport and woke up refreshed and ready for our night-time adventure of dinner and friends.

She is so smart and well-behaved. I am glowing with pride and adoration. She is so beautiful and kind, so sweet and creative, so gentle and strong. I love her more and more as time goes on. My heart is expanding again and I am resting into the perfection of our little family unit. We are so good together. We really know how to meet and anticipate her needs.

This trip is an amazing opportunity to get out of our routine and enjoy each other. Moving to Bend was so intense—we slammed right into a full life without much breathing room. Now, we get a chance to reflect and sink into connection without our usual distractions. This is day two of seventeen days of travel.

Following that perfect travel day and nourishing evening, today was the best day I've had in a long time. I was joyful and my anxiety stayed far away. We went on a public transit adventure together through the big city and it was perfect. My daughter was in heaven as we navigated busses, trams, and gondolas for her first time. She sang and laughed as we strode across a huge pedestrian bridge that went over a multi-lane freeway. She oo-ed and ah-ed at the view at the top of the gondola ride that showed us the Portland cityscape from above. She yelled "Faster Daddy, faster!" as we ran around gardens full of lush plants that can't be found in our High Desert home, strapped to her father's back with me trailing behind taking photos. She fell asleep on him as we floated down the gondola and searched for the right tram to take us back to our rental apartment.

My husband and I sat holding hands and smiling the whole ride back, enjoying the peace and togetherness. She stayed asleep as we walked through the dense city streets to our place. We stopped in a fancy Asian tea house. I bought some Pu-erh, my favorite kind of tea. It is aged and musty, smoky, earthy, rich. When we got back to the apartment, she was just waking up. I put on a pot of tea and my husband and I drank it out on the front porch in a little patch of sunshine while she had juice. It was warm enough to take off our jackets. My daughter padded around the deck barefoot. We drank tea and listened to music, took in the warmth of the winter sun, and danced together.

Pleasure gushes through my brain and out my eyes as I look at her and feel us all together. Ripples of bliss emanate from my head and make me blurry-eyed with pleasure. The bursts of oxytocin are palpable, noticeable, impactful. Something beautiful is happening within me. I really like my role right now. I like my life. I like my little tribe. I like being so present and fulfilled. I like not striving or trying or getting frustrated in the not-having. I like not worrying about how I'm going to create a business or what my purpose is and all of that. I am here now and I love it. I have been fully alive these past few days and the level of love I am accessing is astonishing.

It's rainy and cold this evening, but my heart is so warm. My daughter is asleep and my husband is doing yoga in the living room. I am typing these words and breathing deeply in the bedroom.

This trip is the medicine we all need. I thought it would be hard and disruptive, but it's actually heavenly. We'll see if this continues tomorrow when we take a five-hour plane ride to a different time zone and meet up with three other people. But for now, I am content, satisfied, and so happy to be this me here now with them.

Contentment

It is a good day
Even though
It's not perfect
Or fabulous.

Even though
It's not
Super fun
Or interesting.

Even though
I don't exactly know
What I'm doing in this world
Or where life is leading me.

It is a good day
Even though
My belly is
a bit uncomfortable.

Even though
I didn't get enough sleep
And I really want to
Stretch my legs.

Even though
There is turbulence and
I'm afraid of heights—
Still, I am calm and happy.

This truth
Is proof of my growth.
These facts show that
I am on track.

a moment alone

I am out on a walk by myself—the first chance I've had to be alone since we arrived here in Hawaii two days ago. It's been a whirlwind since we landed. Now, finally, everyone is settled and I set out for a walk to explore.

Poetry is flowing out of me. I keep stopping here and there to write in my notebook. I'm a bit worried it's not okay to be scribbling incessantly in front of someone's property using their retaining wall as a standing desk under a big tree, but I'm doing it anyway. I am getting shade from the light rain that is falling. I think a mosquito just bit me, and eventually I have to go back to my family. It's nice to be part of a traveling unit but also challenging to be in close quarters with all these people.

Yet, I am grateful to be here now. The sweet cawing of birds and the lushness of the tress and the perfection of this moment are swirling together with the joy of receiving the space I need. My heart is glowing.

———

The light is dimming—almost time to resume my responsibilities of parenting. But for now, I am alone in a new place and the nature is singing me sweet songs of welcome. I am savoring this time, these precious ninety minutes, to really feel and be with the inspiration of this decadent landscape. This place is penetrating me in ways the pines and junipers of the High Desert never will. They are beautiful, yes, but there is something special here that is trying to tell me something.

I am listening with my whole body and all of my senses. I am pausing and letting the island tell me its precious truths. I am drinking in the sound of the rain and the call of the birds and the smell of the fresh tropical wonderment. Even in this paved neighborhood near a golf course where we are staying, nature is knocking on the door of my heart with something to share. I am listening as best I can in these small moments before I have to jump back into the chaos of family life, back into being the mom of the entire trip—planning and making sure everything goes well and there is enough to eat and we all have fun. It's a lot of responsibility.

I didn't sign up for this role—it just fell on me. My father-in-law is not married, and the other siblings are single and younger than me. Somehow I have become responsible for all the planning and mom-ing. It's a lot to hold. But with the fresh scent of island flora, I am gaining more strength, more awareness, more presence. I believe I can do it all. I can find space within the togetherness to truly hear what this island is sharing with me. I can be responsible for the success of the trip in the role of "Mom." I can do all of that, and stay relaxed and open to receive the gifts of Hawaii. At least I really hope so.

hawaiian nightmare

U p until now our trip has been crazy. When we
arrived, our Airbnb was disgusting. It was dark and
pouring rain; we had been traveling the entire day. The
owner of the place greeted us at the door. He was an old,
fat Russian man in a tattered bathrobe, hairy chest
exposed. He stood halfway in the sliding glass doors,
smoking a cigarette. Smoke billowed out and into the
house. We darted in, trying to stay dry, carrying all our
luggage quickly from the car. When we set it down and
looked around, we were appalled.

The smell of liver and onions wafted around the house,
mingling with the cigarette smoke. The downstairs reeked
of mold, more mold than I have ever smelled. It was dirty,
so dirty. My poor little babe was bone tired from more
traveling than she had ever done in a day. She clung to me
like a terrified monkey as us adults argued in hushed
whispers about what to do.

We couldn't stay there. It was uninhabitable. There
were huge dogs barking outside. The carpet was dirty and

stained. There were medication bottles and pills everywhere, tobacco strewn about. There were huge knives hanging on the walls low enough for my kid to grab. It was the stuff of nightmares.

I carried her around from room to room, panic growing in me. It was way past her bedtime. We decided we had to just stay there for the night, and would figure it out in the morning.

I tried to run a bath, her nightly ritual, but the bathtub was filthy. It was littered with pubes and soap suds and other grime. It all swirled around when I tried to clean it with one hand while holding her on my other hip. I gave up and just got her dressed in her pajamas. "Go in?" She pointed to the little blow-up bed my husband had set up for her. "I go in?" She had never asked to go to bed before, but the poor precious girl was using the few words she knew to try to get to sleep. My heart lurched. Tears sprung in my eyes. A swirl of emotion surged in me. I wanted to protect her from this. I felt powerless. I felt like I failed her. I felt scared. I felt so many other unnamable things. I put her down in the weird little bed, laid down next to her on the dirty ground, and tried to soothe her to sleep. She was out in a few minutes.

———

I stumbled into the living room, rubbing my eyes, turning off lights around the space. It was Christmas Eve on the Big Island of Hawaii. Every single hotel room and Airbnb was booked. It was the busiest week of the year on the island. There was nothing else available. Still, we tried. We frantically searched on our little cell phones, trying to find anything that was open for us to move into the next day.

No luck. Plus it was already past eleven at night, everything was closed.

My father-in-law went to bed. My husband and I stayed up with his sister. She is having a hard time with her mental health lately, so we held space for her, rubbed her back, helped her process her anxiety and feelings and emotions. The situation we were in didn't help at all. She was panicking. So I took the stance of the optimist.

"Don't worry," I declared, standing tall, hands on my hips. "Our job right now is to remain hopeful. This is all going to work out. We are going to experience a miracle. Something better than we ever could have planned is coming."

I took a wide stance, put my arms in the air, and began praying to the island. "Mama Pele, please help us. We need your assistance. We need a miracle. Please hold us and support us in our hour of need. Please grant us safe passage upon your land, and give us a comfortable place to rest our heads so we can enjoy your bounty and splendor." I did some wild twirling witchy dance, stomped my feet, threw my arms down, and said, "It is done."

Sister looked at me skeptically. Husband looked at me with adoration. He is used to my wild prayerful ways that come out sometimes. It had been a long time since I embodied the spiritual confidence to pray like that, and I could tell it made him happy with the remembrance of the power I used to wield. I felt energy surge through me and smiled, remembering my own magic and strength.

It was far out, and the odds were slim, but I truly believed we were going to be rescued by some kind of miracle, though I didn't know what it was. "It will be a Christmas Hannukah miracle!" I proclaimed. "Tomorrow is the holiest day of the year. Christmas and Hannukah at the same time! A miracle is inevitable," said the pagan-witch-Buddhist-sometimes-atheist. "We have to just trust and believe. The island will take care of us. We just had to get shaken out of our comfort zone in order to receive it. Something amazing is on the way."

In that moment, I really did believe it. I had no idea what would happen, but I trusted the magic of the island. Someone had to, so I did. Finally we all went to bed.

———

Even though I did believe a miracle was coming and we were provided for by the island, in that house, I was scared. I didn't know if the sheets were clean. They felt gritty. The birds outside were ridiculously loud. The windows wouldn't close. We probably wouldn't have closed them anyway, even if they worked, because the room was so moldy that my nose stuffed up immediately. When we got in bed, I clutched my husband, wrapped around him like a koala on a tree. Usually we sleep with separate blankets when we can, not touching. This time, I fully encased him, my heart racing, unable to relax. With our limbs entwined and the security of his body holding me steady, I was able to find a resting place and eventually drifted off to sleep.

———

When I woke up in the morning, it was still gross. Everyone got back on their phones, trying to find anything else available. There was nothing. The island was literally booked solid. My husband hopped on Facebook and put out an SOS and also called everyone he could think of that had connections or property in Hawaii. No luck.

I did my best to stay calm, especially for my daughter. I didn't want her to freak out even though we were all panicking. There was no way we could stay in that disgusting and dangerous place the whole time.

I made some breakfast for everyone and we ate gratefully. I tried to not think about what was on the chair I was sitting on, wishing I had put on pants that morning instead of shorts so my skin didn't have to touch anything. I went out for a walk around the jungle neighborhood with my sister-in-law, trying my best to enjoy the beauty, even though we still didn't know where we were going.

The land was lush, dripping with moisture. Tangles of ferns mingled with tall palms and unfamiliar, lush tropical trees all along the road. The sky was spacious and blue between passing clouds. Houses sat far back from the street, hidden in the jungle. Birds called. Bugs sang. The world smelled alive. I reached up and breathed deep, connecting to the life-force of the place, the intelligence that was there beckoning me beyond the filthy house.

———

When we returned, a miracle had indeed happened. My husband's Facebook post was fruitful. An old friend from high school reached out and said her parents had a condo on the other side of the island. They live there full-time, but happened to be traveling that week. They invited us to stay at their place as long as we needed, for free. After some uncomfortable conversations with the owner of the gross house, we got a full refund, packed up our stuff in a mad dash, and jumped in our rental van.

We were heading to the sunny side of the island. All of our spirits lifted. Smiles all around. "I knew it!" I exclaimed. "This is our holiday miracle!" Everyone laughed and agreed. We were off on our real vacation, which started the moment we left that house.

———

First stop: Starbucks. It was the only thing open on our route, since it was Christmas day. We caffeinated and were joyful. Next stop: Rainbow Falls! We got deep into the Banyan tree forest nearby and marveled at the beauty of the waterfalls. True to the name, there were plenty of rainbows and it felt like we were finally getting in the flow of the trip we had hoped for.

We then drove straight across the volcanic island for a few hours and ended up at a beach for a picnic and a dip. My daughter napped in the car, perfect, and woke up right when we got there, excited to play in the sand. It was raining a little bit but not too much, and even with the strong winds we ate outside and played in the ocean.

We got to our new vacation home in the late afternoon. It's a little two-bedroom condo on a golf course. It feels clean enough and safe, well-loved and cared for. Even though it is much smaller than our previous booking, we're making it work. We can cram six people into a two-bedroom condo, sure. We do it happily, now that we know the alternative.

When we arrived, we opened the back sliding doors, which open up onto the expansive green golf course with scattered tall trees. We all stepped outside and felt relieved and happy. The air was fresh and flowing, no mold or cigarette smoke to be found.

The neighbors on both sides came over and showered us with welcome gifts. The owners of the condo had contacted them and told them our situation. They gave us milk, cereal, bread, and PB&J for the next day; they gave us Christmas cookies and treats. They let us know that if we needed anything, we could count on them. Then one of them declared that they had plenty of extra Christmas dinner and would bring over prime rib and potatoes for us a little later. They also invited us to come over after dinner and join them outside on their patio for singing and socializing. We all cried from the generosity and the sanctuary of this place compared to the previous lodging.

———

And now, it's the next night. I am sitting alone on the porch, a gentle glow of string lights overhead. We had a great day of adventuring. We went to the beach and played for hours, had lunch out, and enjoyed our time exploring these new surroundings. Our vacation is finally in full swing.

Everyone else has gone to bed, but I can't sleep yet. I am breathing deep of the clean tropical air. I am listening to the quiet of the night and gentle busyness of the birds. It's warm enough to be out here without a sweater. I'm sitting on the cushioned patio furniture with my feet up on the coffee table. I am unwinding and congratulating myself. I am repeating my prayers of thanks and gratitude for whatever mysterious forces led us to this clean and welcoming space.

———

I held it together that whole time. I carried us on my optimism all the way from dingy and dangerous to a soft safe haven. Now, I am soaking in this solitude and being with my art, centering myself and enjoying this space before a new full day begins.

actually, not enough

It's been five days of family togetherness. I'm losing my cool. All I want is time to myself to truly be with the island and my own creativity. I crave to walk in the jungle with no one else chattering around me. I want only my breath close by, taking in the fresh oxygen, only my bare feet in the soil, absorbing the volcanic energy. I want to unwind my being and receive the information this luscious landscape has to offer. I want to listen deeply with no interruptions. I want to be rained on in peace so I can really feel the gifts of this ecosystem. I want to pray out loud through song and dance and shout incantations into the blowing wind, hearing the whispers in reply without straining. I want to listen to my own thoughts without being interrupted so I can become who I truly am with the help of this island magic.

———

This place is changing me and I need to be present to that unfolding. I can't find enough time and space away to truly let it sink in. Instead, I take hurried sips in stolen moments or find some stillness amidst all the bustling of a big family in tight quarters. I am writing this outside on the lanai while everyone else is in bed, again. The sky is clear and starry. The breeze is warm yet cooling. I took thirty minutes to myself the other day to walk down the beach while they all were playing in the water. I took ten minutes to walk alone through the mountain neighborhood we had lunch in two days ago when the food was taking too long, my eyes hungry for the lush plants and flowers, mind meandering like the motorbike that zoomed by. I wandered barefoot last night through the golf course— dark space, moist grass, big trees, deep breaths. It's something. It's not enough. I am doing my best to harvest what I can while I am here and I also mourn this missed opportunity to fully sink in and transform.

Despite these suffocating feelings arising in me, our time together has been great. We are seeing the sights. We are going to beaches and having nice meals and getting along. I just would have done this trip so much differently if I were alone. I would have spent much more time in the jungle instead of the city streets. I would have had so much sex— the life force here is incredible. The sex would have been explosive, volcanic. There has been no room for that. My husband has barely touched me this whole time and it's annoying, frustrating. It's understandable, of course— we are crammed in a little house with his whole family. But my body is turned on in ways it hasn't been in years. My loins are pulsing from the sensual aliveness of this place. My heart is open from travel and the beauty of the land—but now it is closing the less I have time to actually enjoy myself.

This desire for space alone with the land and myself is not a whim—it's a spiritual and emotional need. It's for my sanity and mental health, my artistry and growth, my wellbeing. I don't know where I will find the time away from the family to have it. I'm angry, sad, grieving. I want to get away from them in order to feel myself, but I also feel guilty and confused. Why do I need to be isolated in order to feel free? Why can't I be fully me in the midst of it all?

alone

I am finally alone. After a week of traveling, finally, my need is being met. I am on a secluded road surrounded by jungle. There are no other humans in sight or earshot. Finally, I can breathe. Finally, I can listen.

It's our last full day here. Everyone was packed in the minivan, ready to go to a morning dance party at a resort close by. It would have been fun. I like those kinds of things. But my skin felt electric, my nerves on fire. If I spent one more day with them without taking space for myself, I would explode. If I never got the chance to quench this yearning for a quiet stretch of time alone with the island, I would regret it forever.

I reluctantly hopped into the middle row next to my daughter. The sliding door closed. My heart started pounding. My skin started buzzing. I was going to have a panic attack. "I change my mind!" I blurted as my husband started the engine. "I can't go with you!" My words were terse and forceful. I was losing it. "Just drop me off at that military road we saw yesterday, the one that's closed to cars. I'll see you in a few hours."

He looked worried for a second. I could feel everyone holding their breath. But he agreed and drove the few minutes to the jungle road we noticed on our family hike the other day. As soon as he stopped, I flung the door open and jumped out. "Bye, honey!" I waved to my toddler. "Have fun!" She looked at me, confused. I forced a grin. "I'll meet you guys back at the house when you're done." I slammed the door.

They drove away. My heart rate slowed. The panic subsided. My vision cleared. I looked around me. I found my balance. The dizziness receded. I smiled for real and took off down the gated road.

It's not the big, dense, wild jungle that I hoped for. It's smaller and paved, not a rooty wet trail. But it's just me here with the tropical birds and the muggy air. I hear the twittering insects and take in the animal sounds from all directions. I am surrounded by life and jungle. No one is around. Not one single person for miles.

I see green and green and more green, different shades and tones and textures, with some speckles of purple and orange flowers here and there. Lava rocks line the road and I saw a big shell back there. Gravel grumbles under my boots as I traipse and meander, soaking it in.

This is all I wanted. Some time, some peace. I was filled to the brim with my husband's family and their incessant chatter about everything not here now. Their noises and chewing and drama and complaints were driving me mad. Finally I am alone with this island and a pen, this nature and my own mind. I feel my whole being healing in a deep, long sigh of relief.

This is what I need. I need space and I need connection. I need aloneness and some togetherness. Both are what make me healthy. Sometimes I most need to lean into bonding, sometimes I need to be autonomous and free. One time a few weeks ago when I had extreme anxiety at home, I needed to hold my baby on my lap for an hour while we watched a movie. In that moment, it was the only thing that quenched my quivering anxiety and calmed me down. Today, this week, I need only the sounds of nature and my own footsteps. No amount of togetherness will do.

I am learning ever deeper about my nervous system and my needs, about bonding and attachment and independence, about how my childhood shaped me and what is wounding versus wisdom. I am learning how to identify and advocate for my needs before I explode from suppressing or overriding them to meet the needs of others. I am arriving at acceptance of my delicate self and the things I must do to have balance and be in a good mood, a stable space, a healthy place.

Too much time alone or too much time together takes me out of whack. I am learning the warning signs in both directions and doing my best to course-correct before I break down. I am learning how to be a healthy, happy human who lives with other people every day and can't escape. I can't run away from my life even when it gets too overwhelming.

I need them, too, even though I sometimes wish I could leave forever. When I'm overloaded, being alone in an isolated place seems like paradise. When I am lonely, being together and doing life with other people seems like heaven. I am doing what I can to take the best from both extremes and find a balance that works for me and my family.

Being here, now, alone and with myself, surrounded by wildness yet safely on the road, I am finding peace.

finally

I am perched on two rocks, going soul to soul with a wild orchid. I can feel the presence of it from six feet away. It stands out like an intelligent alien in the midst of tall green grass and bushes. Vines crawl down the lava rock wall—a patched-together barrier of pieces from a long-ago explosion. The vividness of life here is startling, inspiring, orgasmic.

Here, an orgy of life-force entwines unto itself infinitely. I feel a playful erotic pulse. I revel in this eco-sexuality. The moss is soft and sensual, caressing the road in the sweetest tickle. I bend over and touch it, shivering from the texture, feeling my pussy open, relax and dampen.

The moist air in my nostrils is so fragrant and saturated. I allow myself to be penetrated by its gentle entering. It flows in at the perfect moment when I am ready to receive. I pull it into me, savoring. The sun peeks out from deeply stacked clouds. I lift my face to take it in. I see colors and shapes behind my closed eyes.

Heavenly awakening is happening in my body and beyond, pleasure rippling downward, filling my heart, rooting into the earth. This flowing energy then trickles outward into the body around my body and ever wider, caressing the universe.

I haven't felt this way since long before becoming a mother. I am reawakening to the natural pleasure I once knew. I am filled with palpable gratitude for returning to this state—to feel so connected and take in this much. I thought it was gone forever, but now, here it is, here I am. I knew something important was happening within me because of this island. Now, alone with the land and my senses, I can finally unravel it, unpack it, have it.

I revel in this time of merging with the earth in ever-opening enjoyment. The view of the trees relaxes my soul. The sound of the bugs is like a vibrator massaging my essence into pleasure. All the life around me is a dance of seduction and awe, enjoyment and anticipation.

I lick my lips and carry on, energy flowing, grounded and connected to it all. I breathe deep and sigh out the sound of, "Finally."

fruit feast

On my way back from my eco-sexual awakening, I found huge, ripe passionfruit growing on the side of the road. We moved to the other side of the island two days ago, into a bigger house in a much lusher, wilder neighborhood. I smiled with glee and jumped up to snap one off the vine. My favorite fruit—ripe and there for the taking. It was big and green and the largest I've seen. I carried it home after my delicious hike in my little backpack. When I got back to the empty rental house, I cut it open to reveal the most abundant and juicy harvest. I ate half with a spoon and left the other piece proudly displayed on the kitchen counter for them to enjoy when they got home. Them—my family. Even in my precious alone time I think of them.

Then I got a new plate and piled it with eight longans from the farmers market—juicy little fruits that look like rocks on the outside and taste like gummy candy. I sat on the floor in the airy yet humid enclosed lanai, scoring them open one at a time. I would slice it, then crack the skin apart. The shiny pearl of fruit would rise out triumphantly. I popped one in my mouth and bit the flesh in half, tongued the seed out into my hand, dropped it on the plate with a clink. Then I chewed delicately, luxuriating in the flavor and texture, over and over, eight times in pure pleasure and presence. I love tropical fruit.

———

Earlier in the morning, before my solo excursion, I went on a short walk in this jungly neighborhood and came across a coconut in the road. I picked it up and shook. Slosh, slosh, it was full and good. I carried it home with pride and gratitude, thanking the land for providing such a gift. It was a short walk. When I got home I presented it to my husband and said, "I found this. Open it, it's a man challenge!" We didn't have any real knives at our new Airbnb, so he took a pocket knife and gouged through the rock-like casing, finally boring a hole big enough to get the tasty juice out. I sipped it first in wonder. It was perfect. Not too young, not too old, the clearest, cleanest coconut water I've ever tasted. I took another big gulp and then shared it with the rest of the family. We marveled at the deliciousness. After the juice was all gone, my husband slammed the shell against lava rocks over and over until finally it opened to reveal the fruit. We devoured the flesh with gusto. There is still some left in the kitchen and it tastes just as a coconut should.

———

This land is so fertile and giving. I am blessed and grateful to receive. Soon the others will return to this rented tropical home and we will all be together again. I feel satiated by my time alone on the land. I could definitely enjoy more, but it was enough to feel okay. I am amazed at the sensual, spiritual, energetic awakening I had. I knew there was something happening in me that needed my undivided attention. I could feel the twinges of it on the periphery of my awareness, but couldn't fully sink into it until I was alone. Now, I know that level of sexual energy, that level of spiritual connection, is not gone forever. It's been dormant in me, buried under all the responsibility, busyness, and mothering. But it's not dead.

I am alive in familiar old ways again. I am returning to the truth of myself. I am revived deep in my soul. I am awake to the potentiality of my own bliss, to the profundity of my connection with the universe and nature. I will take this with me, back into my regular life. I will do my best to cultivate this level of awareness wherever I go.

Now though, I will taste some more coconut in the remaining peace and lay down to integrate all the abundance and information I received from the land. I have about thirty minutes left until my family returns and I will do all I can to let this magic sink deep into my cells and stay forever.

hawaii before

There I was, on mushrooms, dancing on a Hawaiian beach at a music festival. I was twenty-six and I was free.

Before that trip, I was living in Oakland. It's a long story, but it was time for me to leave again, like I always did. This time I did it dramatically. I sold my car, broke up with my primary boyfriend, moved out of the house we shared, closed my catering business, and booked a flight to Maui.

I had no plan of what I was going to do there. I had a couple thousand dollars and a little room left on my credit card. I was not concerned with coming back. I thought I might stay awhile.

Really I was chasing a man. We had been on and off for years at this point. We were mostly off at the moment, but sometimes on, and the thrill I got from being with him drove me to follow him to the islands.

That moment on the beach, dancing under a moonless sky, the stars so bright, the tiki torches illuminating the shore, the bass music bumping from big speakers nearby, bare feet in the sand, wind in my short, curly hair, psilocybin in my brain—everything felt absolutely perfect. He was there, I was there, we all were there, and there was the place to be.

The next morning felt a little less perfect. The sun was blazing through my tent, making me sweat. I felt disoriented, strung out. I started to worry about what was coming next.

I popped my head out of my tent, looked around, and stepped out. There he was like magic, handing me a coconut with a straw in it, his signature dopey-eyed smirk reminding me that yes, this moment is divine and we are blessed to enjoy it.

He wordlessly swooped his arm around me, guided me to the shade where he had set out a sarong as a picnic blanket. I sat on the ground and drank the coconut, smiling, as he prepared a breakfast of fresh fruit, nuts, and seeds. He fed it to me by the spoonful; I was googly-eyed and in love.

The rest of the trip went exactly like that. I would start having the feeling that things were actually not so great—an accommodation would fall through, or it would rain hard on us while we were walking with our luggage and we didn't have a ride, or we had no idea what was coming next. Then, a miracle would happen. Something amazing would swoop in and guide us to the next great thing. He and I traveled together for two weeks after the festival, crashing with random hippies in the jungle, running into our friends from the mainland who invited us to stay at their rental house, all sorts of serendipities catching us at exactly the moment we had run out of plans.

Then, something shifted between us. I cried all night and the terrible feeling did not get fixed by some miracle. It was another break-up, another off-again moment of me ripping my own heart out. He was an unconditional lover. I never felt rejected by him; he was always available, even when he was with other women. I was the one that would create a reason we couldn't be together—usually because I couldn't handle polyamory the way he did it back then. There were no rules, nothing to depend on. Sometimes I would find other reasons to leave him or not see him. But I always went back.

He flew out a few days later. I was still there. Alone. With no plan. The sinking feeling set in, but once again not for long. My friend from the mainland took me under her wing, took me to amazing campsites, showed me the best restaurants, hooked me up with weed from the island boys she had befriended. When she left on her flight, she let me use the rental van she had been driving. The island was sold out of rentals that week. I thought I was going to be screwed. Then, another blessing, another miracle. I drove around and slept in the car, checked out all kinds of beautiful places, met more cool people. I was on a roll.

But my money was running out. I didn't have a place to live, or a job, or a community, or any prospect of any of those things. I had just left my huge house in the Bay Area that I shared with a tight-knit community of friends. I was the new guy, the odd one out. Once I left—or fled, rather—all those bridges were burned and I wouldn't go back.

I considered staying in Maui, forging a new path for myself. I had met enough people, I probably could find a way. But then he contacted me. Or I contacted him. I don't know. We made up a little. I wanted to be with him again.

So I booked a flight, returned the rental car, and left.

When I got back to San Francisco, I met him at a dance club late at night. A hit of acid was placed on my tongue. It was a dark and sultry club in an industrial area, multiple rooms, dim lighting. One room was small with red lights and a bar, one was huge with blue, purple, pink lights and a fog machine. I was in that big room, the music rumbling my soul, the LSD taking its hold—expanding all of my senses, fractals behind my eyes. Then I saw him. He was dancing with *her,* the other one, the other on-and-off forever girl. My eyes narrowed. My heart sank.

Just then, a cute guy wiggled by me, carried by the music. Instead of following the sinking feeling of dread, I followed this new guy. Turned out he was an incredible dancer. We moved together for hours, hot and sweaty, gracefully thrashing our bodies all over each other and the concrete floor, pupils giant. All I remember is feeling and sound and movement and perfect symbiosis. I thought I was in love with him—we moved so perfectly together.

Then the night ended and I didn't get his number. It was getting close to daylight. The guy I had followed to Hawaii and back took me home with him to his van in Berkeley. I slept there with him, cuddled up with arms and legs and so much energy. But maybe that's not what happened. Maybe we went to hang out with other people somewhere and stayed the night, a little after-party— everyone cuddling and massaging, laughing and moaning from tantric human touch. I don't remember. I do remember thinking something like, "This is the life. I love this life."

The next day, though, reality hit hard. Somehow in my drugged-up escapades of rolling all over the concrete floor,

I had seriously hurt my knee. It was swollen, throbbing.

My van guy tried to take care of me for a few days, but it wasn't working. I couldn't walk.

I was running out of money, I didn't have a plan, I didn't have a house. I couldn't get around by myself. I couldn't work a job. I didn't have health insurance, couldn't get medical support. So I crawled back to my parents. The fun was over.

I tried to keep following the flow, enjoying my freedom, chasing lust...but it drove me into the ground. I tried to pretend I could keep running forever, keep avoiding responsibilities, keep taking drugs and booking flights and chasing a man that would never truly be mine. But I couldn't. I hurt myself, badly, and I had no safety net—except for mom and dad. So, tail between my legs, I went back to them. They helped me get on my feet. And as soon as I could stand on my own, physically and financially, I ran again, back into the chaos, back to the weed industry—trimming buds on different cannabis farms, a contract worker with no contracts, no security, no plan—and back into the arms of that guy who was really bad for me. I ran right back to a life of uncertainty that I coveted so much.

I have all these glorious memories of being in Hawaii that last time that I idealize. But the truth is, it wasn't very glamorous. It was hard and risky. It was full of chance and heartache. It ended up really hurting me.

This time in Hawaii, all I wanted was a taste of that freedom, a ride on that kind of serendipity train. I did have a bit of it—like when we got our miracle condo to stay in on Christmas day, or when I had my eco-sexual awakening in the jungle our last day. Those were incredible and astonishing. But mostly I got schedules and responsibilities and a toddler to constantly tend to. Less exciting, but better for me.

This life of stability, though hard, is healing. It's healing my lost soul. It's mending my broken future and giving me something to ground into, to work for, to grow from. Even though I lust after my younger years—my last trip to Hawaii with all its hot hammock sex and psychedelic beach parties—I'm much better off now. Sure, I have anxiety attacks sometimes. Yeah, I can convince myself I am miserable. But looking back now, I would choose this over that any day. The man I'm with now is committed to me, cares for me, truly loves me. He's not going anywhere. I know where I belong. I have financial stability. I know where I'm sleeping. I know who my people are. I have a real family, a real home, a real life.

So, even though I didn't dance on mushrooms at a festival and go with the flow of every moment, I still had a beautiful man handing me a coconut ready to drink. And a whole lot more.

a new year

I woke up with a start. *Where am I? Where's my baby? Is she crying?*

No. I relaxed back into the nice, firm king-sized bed with fresh white sheets and closed my eyes. No. It's just us here, my husband and I. It's New Years Day. We are in a hotel room near the ocean in San Diego. My daughter is with my mother-in-law for a few days. We flew in from Hawaii yesterday. We are alone here.

He was still fast asleep, so I gently crept out of bed and into the living room of our suite, closing the bedroom door behind me. I opened the sliding glass and stepped out onto our small balcony. The air was cool and crisp but not frigid. The palm trees swayed slightly in the gentle breeze. I gazed out onto the pool deck and beyond, into the bluffs and hills behind the hotel, taking it in. It's not dripping with life force like Hawaii, but it's pretty. It will do. My little sanctuary. Two nights away from motherhood duties. Two days to do whatever I want.

I turned around to glance at the empty hotel suite. We

have a living room, a kitchenette, two bathrooms, and a bedroom. Incredible.

I laid down in the middle of the rough carpeted floor and did some yoga—slow and deep, stretching and strengthening, then sat and meditated. After a huge and easeful crap I was hungry, so I smoothed my wild hair, slipped on my boots, and padded downstairs to see what was available. No food, but I found coffee and came back up to our room to prepare chia pudding that I brought ingredients for. Now I sit, dining table rearranged to form a desk facing the open balcony doors, savoring the aloneness.

———

My husband is still sleeping and I am grateful for it. I need this space. I need this view and this simple breakfast and this hotel coffee—this stretch of peace.

Perhaps I will always be at odds with the demands of motherhood. Maybe I will always oscillate between loving my life with my family and craving, needing, demanding space. Maybe a part of me will always envy single women who live on their own, knowing full well they don't appreciate their freedom as much as they should. Maybe I will always wish to be isolated in a cabin in the woods and also fear the vulnerability of that solitude. The writer and the mother, the wild woman and the domestic goddess, the freedom seeker and the community craver— perpetually poised as opposites within me. The pendulum swings this way and that, finding joy and then angst, contentment and then longing, relaxation and then the anxiety that comes with needing something other than what is happening. In this moment, I'm okay with that.

———

It's not a perfect world where everything works out the way we want it to. There are real hardships and challenges here. There are sacrifices that need to be made. I am blessed to live a privileged life where I can examine all of this and have my basic needs met, where I can have glimpses of time alone that I later crave, where I am not in danger on a daily basis and have the freedom to live how I wish. I know these are luxuries not everyone is afforded. I am trying my best to appreciate it and use it for healing and good.

The sky is softly colored by white, wispy clouds. My coffee is cooling. My feet are cold. I finished my breakfast. The grounds are quiet. A bird flew by. There are palm trees in the distance. I don't know what the future holds for me, but right now I am good.

My New Year's resolution is to be more present. I open to a life of less striving, more being, less worry, more listening.

This state I am in right now after being on the island is glorious. I feel an inner rest and glow. I feel a deep knowing that everything is all right and a more powerful understanding of how to listen to the guidance of the universe. I pray to stay connected to it as I get further away from my travels and back into the bustle of life.

I feel grounded in belief. I'm not on a spiritual high, bypassing my pain, chasing miracles like I've done in my past. I'm not in despair and apathy, not believing in anything good. I'm just here, with a buoyant heart and solid legs, doing my exercises in the morning and writing about my process, taking care of myself, trusting that my own art and other purposes will unfold in time.

It's a new year, a chance to be reformed. With this last sip of coffee, I pledge to allow a new self to emerge— someone who knows her center, even in the bustle; someone who stays connected to herself and to her family. I don't want to be at war inside myself anymore, fighting against what is, fighting for what I think should be. I aim to be more like a scale, constantly rebalancing. Not tipping over, tug-of-warring or tapping out—but finding a sweet spot of stability again and again, adjusting what is needed, adding and taking away when the moment calls for it with patience and care.

a glow

Last night, here in San Diego, we went to a New Year's Eve party without our kid. I saw old friends that still live here. It felt good to be in a familiar place with some people I know, yet also surrounded by strangers and incredible music. The food was amazing. The ambiance was great. A fire glowed on the patio. Incredibly talented musicians passed through the stage, taking their turn to serenade the scene. My sister-in-law was there with us. It was cozy and intimate, yet big enough to feel like a crowd. I had two drinks. I loved it. I haven't drunk alcohol in over a year.

I felt free and fun, easy and relaxed, in my body and in love with everything that was happening. Midnight came and went without too much fanfare. My husband and his sister wanted to leave and I didn't, the alcohol and the merriment filling me with energy. But after a little postponing and some protest, I went with them into our rental car, back up the coast. We dropped sister off at her dad's house, got a quesadilla to share from a local Mexican spot, and journeyed back to our hotel room, where we promptly passed out into a deep and undisturbed slumber.

Multiple people I connected with at the party remarked on my glow and beauty. They said something was different about me. "It must be the islands," I replied. "I just flew in from Hawaii."

"No..." one woman I have known for many years replied. "It's something else." *It must be the makeup,* I thought. I never wore it before, but now I sometimes paint my face with the illusion of perfectly clear skin and bright eyes. Later she brought it up again. "I know you said it must be the islands, but you really look different. You have changed. It's coming from within you." I thought about it and realized she is right. I am different now. My time in Bend and on the island has changed me. I feel lighter, freer. I don't feel depressed like I did towards the end of my time living here. I don't feel stressed or worried right now. And more than that...my creative energy and spirituality have re-awakened. I feel my true self returning in a way I haven't really accessed since I gave birth.

Despite the challenges I go through and the struggles I have in finding space for myself within all the caretaking, I also have found a new place within myself. It is clear and bright, spacious and beautiful, uncluttered yet full of possibility, free of expectations yet glowing with potential. Outside, I still have to advocate for time for myself, but inside, I am free.

To Be Moved

Let it unfold through me
like water waving in a roar—
Not passive, moved
by the moon and spin and wind.

Water doesn't drive itself.
It is influenced
by the curves of life
and laws of earth.

I too don't want to do.
Let gravity take me
and creation make me—
I want to be moved.

reignited

He pressed me up against the wall. I felt his energy coaxing me, penetrating me. Our mouths were moving in sync, eyes closed, absorbed in the moment. We had spent the whole day together, celebrating the new year. Now night had fallen.

The floor was littered with the remnants of our romantic night. Chocolate pieces, strawberry tops—a plate of scattered, uneaten morsels. We had sat on a blanket on the ground in our hotel suite, quietly, the lights low, feeding each other sensually, not talking, just being and sensing together. We let ourselves moan and eyes roll as we ate; our bodies undulated as we thoroughly enjoyed the platter of sweets I had delicately laid out.

This was far out of the ordinary for us. Our lives have become nearly empty of passion the past few years—nights of love-making replaced with reading books in bed and gentle snoring by ten PM. But yesterday we did it twice.

The second time, our skin was still warm from the sun, a day spent frolicking at the beach. Our tans were glowing in the hotel lights, blood pulsing from two days alone to finally rekindle our flame. I groaned as he plunged into me, still standing, smashed against the hard wall, throbbing, feasting.

We fell to the floor, pushed the plate out of the way, embraced in a wordless dance of wonder. We moved as one, more deeply than we ever had, engulfed in the fire of our love, reignited.

He took my hand and guided me to my feet, led me to the unfamiliar bed, ripped off the blankets, pushed me down. We flowed together until we had our fill, then slept.

part 6

HOME AGAIN

Motherhood Mode

Back in the motherhood mode,
I find it hard to find my thoughts.

Creativity is illusive.

Pulling at the strings,
I try to bring it back but
my mind is blank
and full of thoughts.

Tracking, watching,
    anticipating, planning—
It takes all of me
to do it all day.

Now finally she sleeps
and there is room for
me to fill yet still
I am empty.

a new way

We flew right back into winter after a week in San Diego. Our couple's time at the suite by the beach ended after two nights. We picked up our daughter and spent the rest of the week visiting family and some friends. It was a blur of shuttling my daughter around to see everyone. My husband was back in work mode so he wasn't around a lot. I was a full-time mom again with no childcare, coordinating all the visits and meals. I don't remember much.

I do know that I maintained my positive attitude and connection to myself for a few days. The high from my time alone on the island lingered a bit. The joy from reuniting with my husband and our sexuality stayed glowing in my heart, even though our bodies barely touched the rest of the trip. Yet as the days wore on, it started to wear off. The stress crept back in. The anger, the anxiety, the suppression of my own feelings and needs. By the end of the week, it built back up and I couldn't stuff it down, couldn't keep it in my gut. Our second to last night there, the dam broke.

We were staying at his grandmother's house in a room with two double beds, a giant closet, and a bathroom. Pictures of his youth were all over the place; faces of cousins glared at us in the dark. We slept apart. The baby was asleep in the large walk-in closet in the room, door cracked, cozy in a padded playpen.

That night, I called him over to my bed. I was worn out from mothering alone all day, again. From navigating his large extended family. From not having any time alone. He climbed into the small, stiff bed with me. "What is it, honey?" He wrapped his arms around my soft body.

"I can't do this anymore," I gasped. "It's hurting me." I started crying. "I need more help. I need more time to myself."

"Okay," he reassured me. "Okay," and stroked my arm. Once I calmed down and wiped my face, he said something like, "I'll help out more the rest of the trip. I'll take Eva over to my mom's tomorrow in the afternoon and you can have some time. And when we get back she'll go back to school and you'll have your half-days again. I'm here to help you. We have help. It's just been a hard time this last week. It will all be okay."

I ignored his optimism. "It's not enough." My chest heaved, threatening hyperventilation, on the verge of a panic attack. "It's not enough," I cried again, moaning, shaking a little.

In the early days of parenthood, he used to be with her more. He was like her other mom. He would wake up early and be with our baby while I got some much-needed sleep. He took some afternoons off to play with her and take her out on walks so I could have some peace or work with the few clients I managed to maintain.

But now, he works all the time. I'm grateful for that. I truly am. He works hard and long hours to provide for us, and I work long and hard to take care of the house and the kid. With this arrangement, neither one of us is really satisfied. He wants more family time. I want more work time. We haven't figured out how to pay the bills and keep the domestic duties done without this strict division of labor.

After a week of non-stop child-rearing, my island enlightenment had worn off. My travel bliss that started in Portland was far away. I no longer felt spacious and free inside. I felt trapped, scared, stuck in a life I no longer wanted yet had to continue living. I couldn't find my peaceful self, my hopeful self, that optimistic woman I was the week before. I couldn't feel my spiritual connection, my creativity, my sexuality. It was just doing, doing, doing all the time with no more time for me.

That night, we made a decision. After whispered conversation late into the night, after I cried some more and shook and moaned, we decided to put our daughter in daycare longer—until three PM each day.

I saw a glimmer of hope. I felt relieved that he heard me, saw me in my plight, sensed that it would be better for all of us if I had more time alone. Finally, I would have my days back. I would be able to both cultivate my sanity and work on something. I might actually have enough time for it all.

We found a long pause in our conversation. Everything had been said. We both yawned. I rubbed my eyes. He kissed me goodnight, climbed out of my bed and into his own. Satisfied with these new changes, calmed by the possibility of having a life I would enjoy, settled by the feel of my husband's strong arms holding me and then the warm spot he left around me, I drifted off to sleep.

back home

ack in Bend. Back in our house. Back to a mess of things everywhere. Back to an edging of overwhelm. Back to an unsettled feeling in the cold. Back to a nagging uncertainty of what to do, to make, to be, to create. But even as all those old familiar things are resurfacing, I also feel a deep clarity and presence. I feel my witness watching, bringing me back to here and now. We've been home for a week and a half.

This morning I cried while stirring my morning drink. Fat tears fell. I am depressed. Not so bad. Not full-bodied and completely. But my heart is sad and my body is confused. It's been snowing for days. Some moments I can find incredible beauty in it. Other times, it weighs on me.

For a few days after returning from our trip, I felt strong again. After crying it out and coming to a solution with my husband, I felt some peace return. Even though I have still been in too much mom mode—our daughter not yet starting longer school days—I stayed steady.

Then, as the days went on, I could feel the corners of

the sadness pulling on me, the overwhelm piling up. I know things are changing soon, but they haven't yet. We had to wait a few more weeks for a spot to open up in afternoon daycare. More space for me is coming very soon, but not yet.

This morning I stayed in bed as long as I possibly could. It's the weekend, so I deferred my parenting duties to my husband. I slept and slept. When I finally got up, I felt bland. I gave myself several orgasms, hoping that would help. It sort of did. At least it got me warm and my energy moving. But as I started my morning routine of drinking electrolytes before inevitably preparing my coffee, the crying happened. I let it happen and was glad. I didn't attach to it. My husband asked, "What's wrong?"

I told him in short, sharp sentences: "I don't want to live in winter. It's getting to me. It's so cold. It's still snowing. I don't like it. And I'm tired of parenting. That is all."

It feels nice to know what is bothering me. To say it clearly without big fanfare. To let the tears fall and be glad for them and then move on with my day. Because truly I am not in some big existential crisis. I'm not having a nervous breakdown again. I have the winter blues. I am worn out from endless parenting. It's simple right now. I know why I feel this way.

I met with one of my new friends yesterday. We walked on the river. The crisp, cold air was refreshing in her company rather than oppressive. I told her the truth. I spoke slowly, deliberately. I shared about my struggles, my depression, my anxiety. I told her a little about the beauty I uncovered by being alone on the island. I smiled as I recounted my adventures with the tropical fruit, the turn-on I felt by tuning into the energy of the land. She listened and nodded, then hugged me. She thanked me for speaking truly. After I was done speaking, I listened deeply to her. We traded off, both feeling heard and held. We are forging a real friendship. It is a speck of color in the endless white landscape.

I've tried to find a therapist here. I've started seeing many, then stopped. They aren't right. I had the same therapist for five years in San Diego. No one quite compares to her. Every time I find a psychologist and they aren't a good fit, I give up for a while. The hunt is so taxing. The searching, the calling, the waiting for calls back, sometimes hearing from them, sometimes not. Sometimes they are not taking new patients. Sometimes they don't take insurance. Sometimes I meet with them and tell them my whole story and then realize they are not the right shrink for me. It's exhausting. I will keep searching, but I need a break from it again.

I am trying to remember the wisdom I gained from our travels. I miss the me I was back then. I was stressed but vibrant. I was in the flow of life and connected to the earth wisdom. I felt trusting and clear. Now...

Now the snow flurries outside are clouding my vision. My body doesn't want to ground into the earth. It's too cold. I feel my energy recoiling from the environment, which makes me even more anxious than usual. I want to run and punch and scream but also stay inside and be quiet.

I feel both mentally challenged and fine. Even though I am having these issues, I am not consumed by them. I see why these feelings are happening. I understand and am doing my best to be gentle with myself. I have never lived in winter before. We just spent time in warm climates and then came back to endless snow. I did so much for other people on our trip and have not had any time to recover. It's natural that some harder feelings would arise.

I'm tired, though. Sometimes my walking feels like trudging. I want to sleep and rest and do whatever I want for a few days. But I haven't had that.

———

In two days, a whole new chapter starts. Monday will be the first day that she stays at daycare until the afternoon and takes her nap there. I am both overjoyed and afraid. I don't know how she will do, being in their care for seven hours in a row, napping in a room with other kids on a little cot. I'm worried it will psychologically damage her somehow, or she will start hating me, or something bad will happen. She's only a little over two. I'm also worried that it makes me a terrible mom to put my kid in school that long every day when I don't actually have to.

I don't have to go back to work, but I want time to myself. I want a long stretch every day so I can think and create and make something of my life again besides just being a mom. I couldn't do it in the little four hours of school we had before. Even thinking about starting a business in those tiny chunks of time was too overwhelming. I had to just take care of myself, find my ground.

I am not going to rush this time. I'm not going to pressure myself to create something of worth. But...I know it will happen eventually. That's who I am.

Deep down, I want to serve. I want to create to give. I

want to use my mind, my heart, my hands to help people. I don't want to just bask in myself all day forever. I want to use the time to see who I am now and then do something with it. I want to use this immense privilege to give back to someone, to something.

But first comes resting. First comes excavating the deeper layers of anger, sadness, resentment, guilt, shame, everything. First comes finding quiet in nature, listening to my own soul, connecting with the heart of the earth. First comes locating myself again within this busy life and role—then comes doing something with it.

———

So, we're going to try it. She'll be at school from eight AM to three PM five days a week. That means I will have thirty-five hours a week to myself. Of course, not all of that is playtime. I still have a house to take care of and errands to run. But it will be time for me to be in my own head, think my own thoughts, follow my own whims, see where they lead.

When I think about it, I get a burst of glee. Finally, after over two long years, I will have my days back. I will have time to think. To sit. To waste time and still have more time. I will have time to write and walk, to exercise my body and mind. I will be able to sleep in some days and still accomplish stuff. I will have time to plan what I want to create, to listen deeply to my inner world and discover what I am meant to do. I will have time to unfold who I truly am now.

———

Today is the last day of picking her up at noon and being with her for the long eight-hour haul until bedtime. Tomorrow, a new era begins in my life, in our lives. It's been two years since I became a mom and now I will finally have the space I need to care for my own soul while caring for her.

relaxing morning

I am drinking the best coffee I have ever had. It's a dark
roast Kona coffee I brought back from the Big Island—
rich and creamy. The earthy aroma rising from my cup
makes my nostrils flare wider to pull it in. My eyes flutter
and roll—intoxicating. I haven't put anything in it, no
sugar or milk, but it's not too bitter and somehow thicker
than other brews. It's perfect, so delicious. The dark liquid
warms my insides with the tropical aliveness I crave so
deeply in this drab winter weather.

I am sitting and drinking without hurry. I am at my
kitchen table, home alone, staring outside into the cold
white snow. In here, I feel cozy, not rushed to do anything
today. My child is in school for five more hours and I have
time. I have time to think, to dream, to relax, to clean, to
walk, to read, to write, to be myself. I have time to
contemplate and enjoy. I have time to breathe and rest.

———

We plan to buy a home here in Bend in the spring, a few months from now. I like living here, I think. My romantic love affair with this town wore off a bit while I traveled, and now I am more sober-eyed while looking at this place. I don't like the winter very much, at least not for this long. It was novel and beautiful at first, but it just keeps dragging on. I really enjoy the summer, though. I like the people. I'm making real friends. They are close by and we see each other often. My dreams of community are starting to come true. It's a small town, but there is enough culture here to satisfy my needs for adventure, for nightlife, for music and dancing. This might truly be the place we stay for many years—our home. It's not perfect, but no place is—just like no person is in any marriage. There are always things we don't like about the people we love. There are always things that bug us about the place we live. It's a little too dry. They're a little too messy. It's a little too small. It's all a little too...straight. But it's good enough.

Our plan is to buy a house here and then travel to warm places for a few weeks or months each winter. My husband's business is growing exponentially and we can actually afford these things soon. This feels both practical and far-fetched, reasonable and unattainable. In truth, it really is in reach.

It's similar to the feeling I get when I think of having my kid in daycare for this long each day, yet not having a full-time job. I have the freedom right now to take my sweet time figuring out what I want to do for work. I get to have the safety and security of a family, the blessings of having a daughter, but I also get to have five days a week to do whatever I want and need. I get to have the love and the nourishment of a baby girl and wonderful husband, and the freedom to pursue my own happiness, creativity, and life path at a leisurely pace. I get to own a home in a beautiful mountain town and live in the tropics part of the winter. I get to have it all, if I want it. But will I let myself?

There is a creeping guilt that comes in sometimes: a shrinking. It's the guilt of a mother living against the grain of what society says she should do. It's the shame of privilege without service.

My mind snickers, saying I am a bad and selfish mom for wanting to have so much time to myself. I am abandoning my daughter to daycare and choosing my own happiness and wellbeing over hers. And isn't it such a selfish waste to sit in the nothingness and ask for guidance, to pray to be moved, to luxuriate in the spaciousness and not rush or hurry to do or make or fix or cure something? Isn't it wrong to just write poetry and prose and sit next to trees or by the river or walk in nature for hours or stare out the window watching the snow while drinking my coffee in a state of awe?

I am learning and resolving that no, those things are not a waste of time and no, I am not a bad person for taking space to do them. I am learning through experience that regulating my nervous system and cultivating my own peace of mind is the most helpful and productive stuff I can do right now.

I am healing myself from years of burnout. I am finding myself. I am becoming the real me inside this role of motherhood. This is the work I must do now. I don't have to rush or jump to help and heal and change and do something out there in the world just because I have a little more free time than before.

My job right now is to be happy and healthy. My job is to find enjoyment in my days. My job is to cultivate presence and resilience. My job is to explore my own creativity and share it. My job is to embody health and vitality, satisfaction and contentment—even though so much is seemingly stacked against me and wrong in this world.

My job is to enjoy: to make things I enjoy, to be a person that I enjoy, to cultivate relationships I enjoy, to keep a home I enjoy, to live a life I enjoy—despite it all, because of it all.

From that place of inner resource, from that well of true happiness, I will be able to give back to the world and my family in real and sustainable ways. Not from a place of depletion and obligation, but from an inner impetus—a movement towards service because I have so much to give. That's what I am going for with all this new space I have to explore. That's why I am taking time to find myself again, to reinvent myself, to heal myself, to be my real self even in this caretaker role. So I can come fully alive, so I can be useful without hurting myself.

I am undoing the generations of pain that says mothers must sacrifice, that women are alive solely to serve the home and husband. I am healing the guilt, shame, and shackles I inherited and am finding my authentic self within it all. I am here to liberate my female body from the bondage of eons of oppression. I am freeing my mind from the burdens and internalized expectations of what a good woman is, what a good mother should be.

I am laying all of that down and prioritizing myself and my truth. I am paving a new way to be a woman, a mother, a wife. I am letting go of these socialized definitions and creating my own. I am discovering who I truly am in all of this and how to merge my past and future selves into someone that is happy to be alive. I am infusing my life of caretaking with my own essence. I am no longer losing myself in this domestic maze. I am finally carving out the space and time to find the me in motherhood.

rage surfaces

The next day, the rage came. It makes sense because I've kept it in a cage, compartmentalized it in order to show up for my family every day and not hurt them with my ferocity.

I woke up and it was there. First, it was anxiety, pooling in my belly, clenching my breath, making me queasy. It was my morning to sleep in—my husband was taking our daughter to school. I heard them walking around, talking, laughing, preparing breakfast. I heard the cabinets slam, even through my earplugs. I made a sour face and growled from my bed. That's when I knew—this wasn't just regular anxiety. This was anger.

I tossed and turned, trying to get myself to relax or go back to sleep, but it didn't work. The rage was boiling inside me. With every sound they made, it got hotter. Finally I heard the garage door close as they pulled out onto the road. I threw the covers back, leaped out of bed, and growled louder, louder. My hands balled into fists. I started tensing, shaking. I threw myself down on the brown carpet, on my naked hands and knees, only my black underwear on. I started pounding the ground with my fists—gently at first, then harder and harder until I was using my whole forearms to beat the ground with all my strength. More growls and snarls, then screams. There was no story behind it. There was no clear reason. It was just rage about all of it, all of it, everything.

The screaming got louder and shriller and came in waves. I pounded and screamed then rested, then caught another round and went at it again, alternating with animalistic sounds and siren yells that the neighbors could surely hear. I flopped onto my back, letting the emotions overtake me, and had a fit—stomping with my feet, pounding with my hands, flailing around, contorting. Finally, it was done. I laid still and breathed.

The anxiety was gone. My belly relaxed. I felt it rise and fall gently with ease. The anger, the rage, the resentment, the agitation—all of it had left me. I was empty.

I stayed like that for several minutes, lost in a blur of euphoric head tingles and soft breathing on the padded carpet. Eventually I got up, took a long shower, and got on with my day.

I will process the mental layers of those feelings sometime. I will uncover the deeper resentments that are driving my anxiety, that are fueling my anger. But for now, I am just feeling it. I am just letting myself embody it without needing to know why it's there. I am giving it the space to surface and move.

I haven't had that. I haven't given myself that. I've been stuffing down my own experience to try to manage everyone else's. I've been caging my rage to try to protect my loved ones. But it's ended up hurting me, and them. The more I suppress my primal anger, the less space I give myself to feel and embody it, the more agitated I am. The more anxious I am. The more resentments I have. The more I lash out.

This time alone is not just a luxury. It's a necessity for me. I am finally feeling what I have buried in order to cope. I am freeing what I have trapped in order to survive. I am letting go of years and eons of anger. I am allowing myself to rage. I am emptying what has kept me stuck in anxious patterns, what has been in the way of true connection with myself and my family. I am allowing the truth to surface and express. I am freeing myself.

dancing

I was alone in my room. It was night. The heater was on, blowing warmth into my space from the wall vent. The lights were off, dark—except for two tiny candles glowing in the corner. My daughter was asleep for the night. My husband was in his room making music.

I had my headphones on, eyes closed, head weaving around to the melody of the music in my ears. My hips swayed to the beat, arms flowed above and around me, carrying me into a trance. I felt the crescendo in the music and my mind disappeared—replaced with sensation, energy, the feeling of being moved.

I let the current of the moment take me, dancing myself into a spiritual high. My head tingled. My pelvis opened. My heart expanded into fractals and space. My body was no longer a separate thing unto itself. It was swept into the motion of the cosmos, the movement of the planet, the tapestry of everything.

My breath deepened, getting steadier, stronger, more rhythmic. My heart pumped faster. I started to sweat and smile. This was it. This was me in my full spirituality.

Energy surged through me, coursing through my legs, into my torso, out my arms and head. I felt like a live wire, a conduit, a channel. I felt my chakras opening, energy pooling in them and spilling out in pleasure.

My spirit soared with the sounds of the electronic music pumping through my headphone speakers; my body opened and undulated with the creative force of the universe. I was the dancer and the dance, the danced and the dancing, the matter and the energy and the everything and the nothing.

I felt stuck places open with ease, rippling with natural ecstasy. I felt numb spots tingle and unravel, coming back to life. I felt weightless, timeless, goalless. I was essence. Though I was confined to the little space in my room between my desk and bed and closet, I was completely free.

Dancing has always been the way I find myself most clearly. It's the easiest place I can connect to my spirituality. In movement, I feel like my most empowered self. I find the soul beyond my body. I find the power within the moment.

The past few years I was estranged from this simple profundity. I was locked up, locked out of the effortless grace I had found so many times before while dancing. I was trapped in my own body, unable to express the deepest parts of myself.

Over time I found my way to movement again, but only sometimes. Only rarely. Only when the stars aligned and I was able to find the rhythm beyond the routine. But now, my vessel is opening again to the magic of creation. My hips are moving to the beat of the universal drum. My heart is spiraling into dances that take me beyond the ordinary and into the center of myself.

That night last week, in the candlelight, in the glowing love I felt pouring from my pores, I was once again my full expression. I was merging with the great beyond. I was fully actualized, fully realized, fully connected again and it felt like heaven. I had found my groove.

two weeks free

M y daughter has had longer days at school for a full two weeks. I feel so much healthier. My mind is more spacious, my body relaxed. It's less challenging to feel my feelings and process them in the moment. I am healing deeply in ways I didn't expect.

I have more time for movement, for walking, for dancing. I have more time for being.

The other day, laying on the floor, staring at the ceiling, tears started to fall. I was taking long, slow, deep belly breaths, in and out, in and out. I had two more hours to myself before I had to get her.

I had spent the morning writing poetry—the kind I will never show to anyone, the kind that makes my soul sing, the kind that is a little secret, just for me. The kind that takes my thoughts and fears and feelings and throws them on a page in a form that may never win awards but helps me heal and understand myself deeper. It was satisfying and made me smile. Then I went on a long walk in the nature preserve near our house.

The sun was shining beautifully, illuminating the snow that fell several days ago. It had an icy crunch in the hard parts and a sensual slosh on the melted pathways. It wasn't freezing outside but still quite cold, so I bundled up in my big jacket, hat, and boots and kept my hands in my pockets most of the way. I barely saw anyone out there that day. The solitude was sweet. I walked with a subtle smile on my face as I listened to lo-fi instrumentals in my headphones.

At one point I came to a big clearing. The sun was strong and direct. I took off my sunglasses and let it shine on my face, eyes closed. I wanted more. I unzipped my jacket and lifted my shirt, exposing my tender belly flesh. I tucked the sweater up over my breasts so it stayed on its own and let my hands down to the side, shoulders rolled back. I lifted my chin, expanded my chest, and stretched my palms out, making a low "v" with my arms. I felt strong, proud, capable—triumphant, even. My subtle smile spread to a full-on grin, teeth exposed. I breathed deep, smelling the crisp winter air with a tinge of fireplace smoke coming from somewhere far away. I stood like that for several minutes, soaking up the sun, feeling empowered joy, being in the moment.

Eventually a strong wind came through and I shivered. I let down my shirt and zipped up my jacket, shimmying my shoulders and making the silly blubbery sound with my lips that comes involuntarily sometimes when I get too cold.

I felt satisfied, so I walked home, more present to my steps, taking in the colors that drew my attention in the neighborhood. A red door. A green truck. Purple flowers painted on an empty garden box.

—

When I got inside our quiet house, I stripped off all my outer layers and flopped down on my back on the carpet in my bedroom. I ran my hands up and down a few times, like a sloppy snow angel, feeling the soft bristles of the floor. Then I placed one hand on my chest, one on my belly, and breathed.

After a few minutes, I felt emotion welling up. Rather than pushing it aside or feeling worried about it, I let it come. After a few more breaths it surfaced and slipped through my eyes, silent tears falling. My chest clenched and then quivered, a wall inside my heart dissolving into tender energy. I tried to just let it be but my mind moved to identify what was happening. It was not sadness or pain. It was relief and gratitude. It was the melting of what I've been through the past several years. It was a sweet mixture of pleasurable release and nostalgic grief—a letting-go, a thawing of the hard shell I had to become to get through it all, now able to finally let it crack and fall away. This went on for several minutes and I was glad. Some tears fell sideways into my ears and I shuddered. I sat up and blew my nose, then let some more fall straight down. I licked one and relished in the salt of my aliveness. I was finally feeling. I was finally healing. I finally had the space and time.

—

The next hours went by both slow and fast. I sat in that liminal space of emotion for as long as I could, trying my best to not think, just feel, not distract, stay with it. I took off my pants and moved to my bed at one point, burying myself in blankets. I rolled around sensually, slipping my legs against themselves and the soft sheets, nuzzling my head and shoulders into the pillows that smelled of laundry and my own musk. I felt like I could have stayed there for days.

Alas, the day had passed and it was almost time to pick up my daughter from school. I got up, yawned, and stretched. Instead of rushing and cursing like I often did, I was slow and wide-eyed. I was gentle and present as I gathered my things. I had tumbled open all day and was full of my own love.

When I got through the door of the daycare, she ran towards me. "Mama!" She laughed and flung herself into my arms. I am still getting used to that kind of greeting. For a while she was so aloof when I picked her up, hesitant. Now she smiled brightly as her teacher helped her put on her shoes.

"She did so great today!" the teacher cheered as I signed her out on the clipboard. "She fell asleep so easily at nap time and woke up really happy. She didn't fight with the other kids today at all. We did some finger painting. It was a great day."

I beamed with relief. I swooped up my sweet girl, said thank you, and headed out the door.

"How was your day, honey?" I asked her in my sing-song mommy voice.

"It was doing great!" She hugged me closer and nuzzled into my chest. In the past, when I would pick her up after being in a terrible mood and stressed out for days, she would sometimes run away from me when we got out the door. It would take minutes, sometimes half an hour of following her around the neighborhood before I finally convinced her to get in the car, and often not peacefully. But not anymore.

Now, when I pick her up, I'm relaxed and so is she. I'm happy to be there with her and she is, too. We delight in each other, a symbiotic relationship. The more I am able to care for myself during the days and defrost all my long-held resentment and emotions, the more she is comfortable being with me. We still have our moments of tension, of course. She's two. Tantrums are part of her development, and so are testing boundaries and saying no. But it's not like it was before. Everything is smoother, happier, less crunchy and sad. It's better for both of us that she stays at school longer and I have more time alone. It's healing our relationship from years of hardship.

———

With this new arrangement, I get to have enough time to care for myself and enough attention to truly care for her. I get to nurture my creativity and feel my feelings so I can actually hold space for hers. I get to have enough time to resource myself and regulate my own nervous system so that when I am with her, I can be fully with her. No longer do I just stick her in front of the TV for hours so I can sit in my room by myself and breathe or clean the kitchen. No longer am I an extremely short fuze, quick to explode when she provokes me. No longer do I half-assedly play with her, my mind somewhere else, barely paying attention, counting the minutes until I can stop. When I am with her, I'm really there. When I'm alone, I'm really there with myself. Things are changing in remarkable ways, all because I finally let myself have what I truly need to feel healthy and alive.

———

There is a small part of me that still feels guilty, that says I should be with her all day like those other moms. But that voice is getting smaller and laughable. Why would I choose to stress myself out and stretch myself thin every day, compromising my mental, emotional, and physical health, just to live up to some strange ideal that exists out there somewhere? I'm not that mom. I've never been that mom. I'm not the mom who thrives on constant connection with my kid. I'm not the mom who completely sacrifices my sense of self and wellbeing in order to be fully attached and connected at all times.

I'm a mom who needs space and time to herself. I'm a mom that needs breaks from kid-land to be with adults and do adult things. I'm a mom who needs solid sleep, alone in my own room, even without my husband. I'm a mom who is so loving and present with my child when I have time to myself. I'm a mom who thrives with her two-year-old in daycare for most of the day, and that's okay. I am coming to accept that it really is okay. In fact, it's great.

Now is the time to cultivate my inner being. Now is the time to get really strong and sure—to practice, to write, to reflect, to meditate, to feel, to rage, to exercise, to create in the comfort of my warm home or a coffee shop. Now is the time to let the long-held tears fall in sweet self-compassion. Now is the time to see who I am with all this spacious time.

glee

I skipped through the patchy snow, singing. Me, skipping. Me, singing. I haven't done either of those things in a long, long time. I laughed as I saw a squirrel scamper away and climb up a tree. I relished the light wind in my face, the stark cold against the warmth of my bundled and mobile body. I stopped in a clearing and caught my breath, then sang some more.

New music is coming to me, coming through me. I used to write songs and sing all the time. Long before I got deep into writing, singing was my thing. It was my therapy, my communion with the Great Beyond, my contribution to the world, my art, my passion, the spilling over of my essence into this material reality. I even recorded and released an EP of original songs one time, years ago. Lifetimes ago.

After my daughter was born, my song went dormant. I've had a few little diddies come through here or there. I've mumbled little melodies to her for comfort or sleep. I've sung the occasional cover song or resurrected one of my old ones on guitar, but barely. Hardly. Almost never. I figured it was just not a part of me anymore. Maybe I outgrew it. Maybe it was stupid anyway. Maybe I was never any good so it didn't matter.

But now, all those negative thoughts—all those sad excuses—have flown away with this fresh winter breeze. My voice is open, my heart is singing, the songs are flowing—old and new ones, fully formed ones, and just passing through ones. I make them up or maybe they use me to be made. They lift my chest and stream from my throat with a natural grace. I feel like an open channel, a creative well-spring.

Comedy is coming through me, too...something I didn't expect. I've never been a comedian before. Sometimes I spend hours in the evenings doing stand-up in our master bathroom. I look myself in the eye and deliver the most delicious one-liners. I'm starting to craft a set, to imagine a show. I think I will perform something in the spring.

This is all strange and surprising. I thought I would write a book and start a business with my newfound free time. I thought I would continue being mostly the same, just calmer and happier. But huge awakenings are happening within me. My creativity is alive in ways I didn't know it could be. I am becoming someone entirely new—animated, funny, full of zest and child-like wonder.

I have tapped into a seemingly endless stream of creation and it is delighting me to the core, tickling my insides with astonishment. I am able to feel glee, actual giddy glee...something I had forgotten the meaning of. I am being birthed into someone I don't recognize but almost remember.

I go to comedy improv night once a week and laugh with my friends. I'm so good at it, too good sometimes. It's natural. I go to a singing circle that is held every month. We merge our voices like sirens, harmonizing on the fly, making up songs together, letting the impromptu melodies guide us. My voice sometimes dances on top, louder and stronger than all the others, able to weave the group sound into an even more potent song. People stop me after and tell me how amazing my voice is. I try to be humble. It's not about that. But it does make me smirk inside and feel great about myself.

I go to Ecstatic Dance one evening a week and fully unleash my glory through movement. I writhe on the floor, spin in effortless circles, undulate in primal ways. I let loose and allow the momentum to carry me into shapes and gyrations I could have never planned. I fall into improvised dances with other people, astonished at what happens when our bodies and energies merge.

This is all beyond comprehension, beyond what I had planned. Something that has been dead and buried inside me for so long is bursting through the snow. My eyes are ablaze, full of light and color. My body is alive, moved by primal life-force. I am awakened from my slumber.

I used to feel like this, when I was in my twenties. It's different, though. I was diagnosed with Bipolar II back then. I've since been re-diagnosed with anxiety and depression, not Bipolar. It might seem that I still struggle in a Bipolar way sometimes, with the ups and downs. Maybe that is what is still going on in my brain, making me hyper creative right now. I like to think it's because of all the healing I have done, all the feelings I have felt in the last month, all the space I've emptied for something new to emerge. I actually don't know. But I do know that it's different now.

Before, I was ungrounded, untethered. The momentum of creative musings would carry me away from responsibility and into trouble. I would neglect earthy reality and chase the high, losing track of my finances, losing a sense of place and home. These days I am weighted, legs solid. I am here, fully here. I am showing up in my daily life. I am caring for my family. I am not blowing away with the breeze of new ideas. I am channeling them, rooted like a tree that is blooming with fresh, fragrant flowers. I am becoming something I have never been.

I stretched my arms wide in the clearing, spinning in a few slow circles, breathing in the nature. It was a cloudy day. The sky was gray, the ground was white, my clothes were black from head to toe. The trees were dusted from yesterday's snow. Everything was dark, muted, dim, bland. But inside, my heart was rainbows and prisms. My throat, the channel for the color to emerge as sound. My vocal cords vibrated with some ancient modern song. The words were an impromptu prayer. The melody was a massage to my soul. My voice got louder, stronger, clearer, truer. I felt my aliveness swelling and emptying through me, filling the space around me, seeping into every cranny of the small patch of forest.

Then, the song ended. All I could hear was the wind and my raging heartbeat. I stood there for minutes, tasting the silence. Then I laughed out loud by myself in the woods. One short burst of giggles. I put my hands in a prayer position and bowed to the nature around me. "Thank you, thank you, thank you." I smiled. I looked around one more time, taking in the space that held me to sing such a beautiful song, then skipped along in the direction of home.

How Dare I?

How dare I
Be so radiant and colorful
When the world is painted
White and drab?
Dreary snow clouds the air
Shrouding even the simple hues
Of brown and green around.

Piles of powder line the ground:
Black turned grey
And grey is white—
Everything, blurry.
The weather is working
To bring me down
And dust me colorless, too.

Yet I walk sure-footed,
Careful not to slip on ice,
Marching through it,
Choosing to dance onto
The softer parts of snow,
Singing songs of warmth
Into the frigid air.

I want to spill my load
Over the landscapes of snow
Coloring the world
With fresh ideas,
Sparkling the scene with vibrancy

That shakes up all this
Winter uniformity.

I am a spunky spectrum
Of multi-toned aliveness
Longing to tumble outward,
To bedazzle the environment—
Spreading joy for the sake of it,
Living art and making it,
Birthing what I feel inside.

Dare I?

my first book

I sat there, clutching my belly, arms folded, rocking back and forth. It was late winter in San Diego and the weather was starting to warm already. There were flowers blooming everywhere. I didn't look at the color and life. I got up and smoked a cigarette outside on the small porch, fixating on the big gray clouds overhead.

I was living in a tiny studio in my parents' backyard. It had no bathroom or kitchen. I used the main house for that. It had no curtains, even. Just a mattress on the floor, a lamp, a small side table. I kept my clothes inside the big house in my childhood bedroom. I was twenty-nine and I had failed again.

No one was home. Both my parents were at work. My siblings had long ago moved out. It was just me, back from adventures, back in financial ruin, back in a totally unmanageable mental health crisis. I hated myself. I hated my life. I wanted to die but wasn't brave enough to actually kill myself.

I spent my days drinking coffee and smoking, loathing.

I spent my evenings driving for Uber and going to bars to drink or dance. I was making some friends—I wasn't totally alone. But in my state of complete self-hatred, friendship was a strange thing.

I finished my cigarette, put it out in the dirt, buried it under a decorative bush, went back inside, sat down, folded my arms, scowled. I clucked my tongue a few times, disoriented by the flavor in my mouth. The back of my throat tasted like cocaine, but it had been a week since I'd had any.

Cocaine was not my drug of choice. I rarely did it. I dabbled in college but never really liked it enough to get into it. Thank goodness. But when I was on a bender or didn't care about life enough, I'd say yes if someone offered it to me. Weed was my drug of choice. It had been for a decade. Alcohol a close second, though I'd go in and out of it. Sometimes I'd stop drinking for years without trying. In my late teens and early twenties I binge drank all the time. But at that point, living in the studio shack, thinking of ways to die, seeing blood behind my eyes—I'd have a few beers or a whiskey or two and call it a night. The week before, though, cocaine was in the mix.

My mind fixated back on the taste in my mouth, my throat. Maybe it was just bitter from all the coffee and nicotine and barely any real food. Or maybe it really was the leftover coke that was lodged in my nasal passage finally dripping its way down.

Suddenly, creative lightning struck in my brain.

I yanked my computer off of its charger and hurriedly stepped out the door to sit on the porch again, machine in my lap, hunched over, typing fast.

"The back of my throat tastes like cocaine. It was a

week ago that I did it. Still, the bitter drip remains..."

My fingers darted over the keys, words appearing in a frenzy of inspiration.

An hour later, I looked up, looked around. I had written thousands of words. Beautiful words. Heart-breaking words. Words so dark and disgusting and hopeless that they were incredible art. *I'm writing a book,* I thought to myself as I reread some of my frantic scrawling.

I had made art out of my suicidality. I had made beauty out of the hardest moment of my life. I had given myself somewhere to put it, something to do with it, meaning to make out of it. I was no longer in a dark and endless hole. I could see the light at the end of the tunnel. I vowed to keep going. I would write this thing every day and make it a book.

I looked around in a moment of awe, realizing that my lifelong dream of becoming a writer was actually happening, there and then. I saw the daisies, yellow centers smiling. I saw the roses budding. I saw hope. I saw life.

I shut my computer and packed up to go. I was meeting a new friend at a hiking trail and was already late. "Sorry, I'm running late," I texted him. "I was working on my book and lost track of time."

From a nobody without direction to a budding author. From a girl who wants to die to a woman with something to live for. From an endless pit of despair to a glimmer of hope, a spark of joy. Writing that book saved my life.

writing heals

I never published my first book. I still have it in a little file on my computer, saved to the cloud. It's there, waiting. I thought I would put it out there but never did. I tried to find an agent a few times with no success. I thought about self-publishing but let it go. It doesn't matter, though. The writing alone was enough to heal me, change me, help me through my hardest time.

I'd like to bring it to the world someday. I don't know if I will. It was so long ago now. My writing style has changed. My perspective on life is different. But I did it, I finished it. I wrote it and edited it and put my loving attention on it. I feel proud of it. The writing is good, though jagged. It's fitting for who I was back then, what I was going through. It ends on a hopeful note. It supported me to heal when I didn't know how. It's a time capsule, a relic.

I did publish my second book. I wrote it during the second biggest mental health crisis I've been through, in my first year of motherhood. *Postpartum* was another book that saved my life. When I couldn't understand what was happening inside me, when my life was a blur of panic attacks and endless parenting, when I was lost and devastated and traumatized, I wrote those words and found my way through. By writing, I made sense of my life, made meaning of my struggles and came back to health. Six months after I finished writing, I self-published *Postpartum: A Story of Unraveling and Becoming.*

Putting that book out there helped a lot of other people, too. It gave mothers a reflection, a blueprint for getting out of Postpartum Depression and Anxiety, an example of another woman who had suffered through the depths and found her way to hope and joy again. I had a little success with it. I got a little press. I sold a couple hundred copies. I got five-star reviews. But more than any of that, I had finally reached my goal of being a published author.

I wrote to heal myself, to feel myself, to find myself, and grew into a woman I admired. I was accomplished in a way I had longed for for years. All my incessant scribbling in notebooks, all the creative writing classes I had taken, all the years I spent dreaming of being a real writer someday had come to fruition.

It wasn't easy. It's not easy. It's hard to prioritize creativity when my world is falling apart. But its the thing that saves me every time.

Now here I am again, writing my way through the dark, finding my voice when I feel powerless, discovering my truth through typing these words, and committing to creating instead of self-destructing. And I did it. I'm doing it. I'm almost done.

I've taken my apathy and turned it into art. I've taken

my loneliness and heartache and put it on a page. I've turned my despair into hope by writing and writing and writing my way through it.

I hope these words will help you too. I hope they inspire something in you. I hope they help you let go of guilt and cultural expectations so you can find your own truth. I hope they will give you a spark in the dark, a recognition of what you can do to light up your own soul, a feeling that you are not alone in your struggles and that you can heal and find yourself too. Maybe it's through writing, like me. Maybe it's through pottery or painting or dancing or a community group or business or starting a non-profit. Maybe it's just through carving out a little more time and space for yourself so you can feel and hear your soul in all the busyness. Whatever you do to find your way home to yourself, I hope this book helps you to do it. It sure has helped me. Writing has saved me once again.

The Making

When my life feels meaningless
And every day is getting
More and more mundane

I pick up the concept of creativity,
Stare at the emptiness,
And make something.

The making brings meaning
To the endless birthing and dying
And gives me something to exalt.

I made this thing!
These words, strewn together,
Hold up my world with hope.

In doing the art
I stretch beyond despair,
Engaging in the now with interest.

While making, I am transformed
From someone who doesn't care
Into someone who does

And this simple process
Has rescued my life
Over and over again.

the me in motherhood

S ometimes I don't know how to fit all this joy into the confines of my life. Sometimes it seems to merge effortlessly—going from skipping in the woods to picking up my daughter to playing with her until dinner time and the whole evening routine.

But sometimes it's like a crash landing—spending the day in my own enjoyment and then forced back into motherhood mode, navigating the realities of a toddler, holding space for tantrums, playing baby games I don't enjoy, bored and flustered by the whole thing.

Sometimes I still feel resentment and anger. Sometimes I still feel anxiety and depression. Sometimes I feel sadness and regret. Sometimes I still wish I had never signed up for this path, never let life take hold in my womb, never said yes to marriage.

It's not all rainbows all the time. I wish it were. I wish I could follow my whims into wonderland and stay there. But that's not what's happening. I am here, washing the dishes, doing the laundry, shifting poop from the baby potty to the toilet. I am here on the weekends, mothering all day, doing the family-time thing. Sometimes the joy from my alone time carries through and it's wonderful for all. Sometimes, I hit a wall and my face falls back into a familiar scowl.

I'm learning. I'm climbing high into possibilities and then stooping down to pick up legos. I'm singing songs of enchantment and then mumbling lullabies out of obligation. I'm accepting that this is how it is and how it will be from here on out. There is the personal unfolding, the excitement in rediscovering myself and there is the responsibility, the planning, the need to show up every day for someone else.

It's good for me though, I think. It's keeping me grounded, balanced. It's making me keep one foot in routine while my insides soar with untethered aliveness. It's making sure I don't run away with the creative current and hurt myself or someone else by tripping, falling because I didn't notice the roots and rocks and branches. It's merging the muse with the mundane, the miracles with the mothering routine. It's making me into someone who can hold it all—astonishment and boredom, hedonism and the humdrum, creativity and commitment.

It's a strange dance, but I like it. It is hard at times, but it's shaping me. I am melding my past with my present, my freedom with my family life. I will never be the untethered maiden I once was, but I feel her here. She is re-emerging as part of me, included in my personal tree. She has been resurrected from a grave I buried her in so I could learn how to be a mother. Now, she rises in my heart and fills in the gaps of the foundation I have created. She bursts forth as flowers in the concrete. She is part of me again, but not like ever before. I am learning to integrate who I was with who I became and who I am becoming. I am not one part of this puzzle of self—I am it all, merged together and growing into something new. This is the Me in Motherhood.

open

I heard a gentle knock on my bedroom door. I was just settling in with a book, covered in my huge down comforter. It was a challenge to put my daughter to bed that night. She fought sleep as long as she could. I was feeling a bit worn out but still happy. I had a great day of creativity and nature time to myself and was still inspired.

The knock-knock surprised me. "Yeah?" I replied quietly.

My husband poked his head in, then tentatively stepped through the threshold. "Hey, honey."

"Hey." I looked up from my book with just my eyes.

"Can I come in?"

"You're already in."

"I mean in there." He gestured to my bed.

I shrugged my shoulders. "Okay," I said tentatively.

He timidly walked across the room and crawled into my bed, cuddling my side as I stayed centered, laying on my back. Things had been tense with us lately.

I was finding myself again, for real this time, but my

explorations didn't include him much. As I was growing closer to my own health and happiness with my new free time, I was growing farther away from him. The resentments in our relationship were becoming more transparent. The things that didn't work were glaringly obvious. I was no longer drowning in a soup of too many feelings I couldn't figure out. I was getting clearer on who I am, what I want, what I need, and what I could no longer tolerate.

He nuzzled into my neck. I winced a little bit. I wanted to be open and connected to him. I wanted to relish in his love and devotion. But in that moment, I didn't. Most of the time, I don't anymore.

He is so supportive, always. He tries his best every day to juggle everything—to work hard enough to provide for our family, to be the best dad he can be, to try to be there for me. But with all those balls, something usually falls short—our relationship. He is incredible with our daughter. He is rocking it at work. He is great at making friends and forging community. He has integrity, humor, an inner beauty that shines through his eyes. But the passion between us had dwindled. The depth of intimacy I desire in my partnership was missing. We had become a shell of a marriage.

That night, we talked about what to do about it. I tried my best to not be cold and snappy, my go-to coping mechanism to cover the deep disappointment I felt about our shallow relating. It still came out, though—I couldn't help it. I could tell it hurt him, but I couldn't stop myself. Since we got back home, since those two nights of bliss in that hotel room in San Diego, we hadn't made love at all. It had been over a month. His body was like a stranger to me. I felt hardened against his touch.

We decided to find a couple's therapist. We needed help. We didn't want our marriage to end, but it was clearly not working. I was growing and changing in so many ways; I was finding my truth and passions again. I was blossoming back into an erotic woman connected to herself, one who has clear needs and desires, but he wasn't meeting me there. Yes, we were great friends. We always have been amazing friends. But the eros wasn't flowing, the intimacy wasn't there, the depth and the "in-love" feeling was missing and I couldn't take it anymore.

Since that night a week ago, things have gotten a little better. We are both making more effort. We have tried sleeping in the same bed a few times as a way to reconnect. We had our first session with our couple's therapist. She is kind and listens deeply. I think she will help us. We have created a schedule for love-making, to be sure it happens. It's so awkward to plan sex. Something that usually is so spontaneous is now reduced to a date and time in our calendar. But it seems to be working a little bit. It's helping us prioritize our connection.

We are also starting to open up our relationship. I met a man...one that stirs the depths of me. One whose touch reaches into my soul and brings forth the electricity inside. One who can meet me in depth of conversation, depth of dance, depth of erotic charge. Not much has happened yet. We've made out and rolled around in sensual bliss. It's been amazing, enlivening, inspiring. But we haven't had sex yet. My husband is open to it. We are all going to meet tomorrow to talk about things, to figure out how this would even work. I have ten years of open relationship experience, before I got together with my husband. He doesn't have any experience with polyamory, but has been curious for years. It was always part of the conversation of our relationship, yet neither of us have considered acting on it until now. The other guy has a lot of experience, so he is really supportive of our relationship and good at communication. That helps.

Just the thought of it, the possibility of having a lover outside of this home, one who is free from the baggage of our relationship history, free from the burdens of child-rearing, one that is available for deep intimacy and brings out the true pleasure in me...sends shivers of excitement through my whole being.

The woman in me is waking up—the deep feminine. Not the mother who cleans and cooks and slaves and starves herself sexually. The sensual, amorous, passionate woman who craves connection, who demands it. I know I need to let my erotic nature live through me. I can't suppress it anymore to try to keep peace in my marriage, and I can't express it fully with my husband right now. There is too much hurt, too much resentment, too much unexpressed pain that needs to be processed in therapy. I can't keep my erotic, creative life-force to myself until we work all of that out. It is begging to be met, to be touched, to be felt and experienced with another.

With every passing day, I get clearer on this: I cannot settle. To do so is to die to myself. To do so is to invite depression and anxiety to take over my being, to possess me with thoughts of death and hatred, to dampen my light and shackle my spirit. I am a full, dynamic, throbbing, thriving human. I am not just a caretaker, not just a role, not just the background to my family's lives.

I am here to forge a new way of being a mother and a

wife. I am here to declare a different way of being alive. I am here to heal the shame and guilt of the generations before me. I am here to release the pain of harmful self-sacrifice.

I will not leave my family. I will not give up on my marriage. I will not abandon my responsibilities, my commitments. But I also will equally commit to myself—to my own happiness, my own well-being, my own joy, my own sexual aliveness, my own needs, my own path. One is not above the other. My obligations to my duties are just as important as my obligation to my own soul.

There are so many ways to do life. There are so many ways to do marriage. There are so many ways to do motherhood. I am staying in it all, but creating my own style. I am freeing myself from the default expectations and finding the ways that work for me. Through making these choices, sharing these truths, living into these explorations, claiming space for my thriving—I am healing myself and my whole lineage. I am breaking free of the tradition of pain and carving a path of pleasurable womanhood—child, husband, family, and all.

like a dog

I walked down the river trail, enjoying the sounds. The water gurgled and rushed. The pine trees swooshed with the wind. It was fairly empty but I could hear people chattering in the distance near the parking lot.

The weather was finally warming a bit. It almost felt like spring. My jacket was unzipped, sleeves rolled up. My arms swung strongly at my sides, moving at a fast pace. The snow was nearly melted, and even as I stepped in the white patches there was no slip, only slush. My boots carved through the landscape with ease.

I had two more hours to myself before I had to pick up my daughter from my parents' house. The sky was just beginning to change, evening approaching. There were a few puffy clouds up above, shifting from white to peach with the setting sun.

I had spent the afternoon at home alone singing songs with my guitar and journaling. Then I drove about twenty minutes to my favorite water-side trail. It is a special place where the river widens and calms. It is lined with grass on both sides, deeply forested. The water is glassy, shining, gorgeous. It's a stark contrast to most other scenes along the Deschutes River, which is often rocky, rough, fast-moving, rapids. This spot is different, special.

I sometimes long to dive in but know it's way too cold for that. I'll have to wait until summer to follow my urge to float down the current, surrender to the force of the river, be taken for a ride by something greater than me.

As I passed a parking lot, a little white dog in a sweater ran up to me and sniffed my legs excitedly, tail wagging. The owner looked up from rummaging around in her trunk and gave me a sideways smile. "She's friendly. She just always has to say hi to everyone."

I laughed. "Oh, no problem, I get it. I have a two-year-old kid at home who does the same thing. She has to greet every person we pass."

She laughed and shook her head adoringly. The dog ran back to her and nuzzled her leg. "Come here, baby," she cooed and lifted the dog to her chest. I laughed again, remembering the dog from in front of the hospital, feeling the whole saga of the past few years bookend before me. Maybe I should have gotten a dog like I said back then, but I didn't. Instead, I got a daughter, a family, and a life full of more love than I've ever known. I got years of challenge and hardship, but a heart of more integrity. I got pain and tears and madness, but I also found this me, here and now. Would it have been easier to have a dog instead of a child? Sure. But knowing what I do now, I wouldn't trade it if I could. Content with my remembrance and realization, I smiled, turned, and sauntered on.

not the end

I wish that was the end of this story. I wish I was free and happy from then on. I wish I had figured it all out and there were no more problems. Unfortunately, the world had other plans. Two weeks after the end of that last chapter, a whole new reality began. The global pandemic of 2020 started and we endured the first wave of lock-downs. My life dramatically changed just a few precious days after I tasted that sweet freedom.

Suddenly, school was closed. I was at home with a toddler all day with no outside connection. The world was a scary and uncertain place. My anxiety went through the roof.

I watched the news and my body seized with fear. I watched my expansive self-discovery halt and crumble. Suddenly, I was a full-time mom again. Our budding friendships and relationships were stripped from us. We had started hosting community events. They were canceled. I was planning a one-woman show, merging song and dance and interactive audience participation.

The dates were booked, the location set. It was canceled. All my free time of joy and skipping was gone. My newfound sure-footedness had slipped away and I was grasping at muddy walls trying to stay upright.

I don't have to tell you how bad it was. You lived through it too. Especially if you are a parent, you understand the depths of desperation and heights of stress those first few months of the pandemic brought on. The uncertainty. The never-ending days. The not knowing when or if things would go back to normal, when or if we would be safe. Stocking up on groceries, trying to be prepared for the complete unknown, trying to keep some sense of normalcy for the family while everything was upside down, trying to keep calm for the sake of the children, trying to make a plan when there was nothing to go on.

The house got messy again. My eyes got bleary again. My temper got short again. My rage piled up again. But this time, it was worse. Not only was I living my absolute nightmare of never-ending parenting with hardly any breaks at all—it all was compounded by the soul-shaking stress of not knowing what was going on in the world and if we would be alright. Not knowing how to create a safe environment for my child. Not knowing what would happen, who would get sick, who would die.

The global and personal grief was immense. There was so much lost, so much changed, so much to let go of and adapt to. I relapsed, hard. I was already smoking weed sometimes throughout this story, and I had those drinks on New Year's, but that was it. Once the pandemic started, it all got out of control. I started drinking regularly again. My weed-smoking increased to all day every day. I was on a crazy ride of substances trying to deal with it all.

My relationship got worse and better. The other guy I had started seeing was out of the picture. Not because of the pandemic—we had some conflicts of interest. So my husband and I clung to each other, came back together because there was nowhere else to turn, no one else to connect with. We spent evenings cuddling or making music, trying to keep our spirits alive, trying to get our needs for touch and love met through our relationship again. We bonded more deeply but our problems also were illuminated more clearly. No distractions. No outlets. Nowhere to escape to. No one else to turn to. Distance couple's therapy helped, but it also brought up the deeper issues. It was a very trying time.

Life was a blur of parenting, processing, pretending things were fine, breaking down in pain. I tried to keep my creativity alive, taking small moments alone in our garage to write poetry, taking brief hikes in the nearby nature preserve. It wasn't enough, but it was something.

I remember walking across the street with my daughter every single day to the tiny park that had only a swing set. It was magically not closed like the other parks, probably because it was so small. I pushed her on the swing for hours. Sometimes she would fall asleep there and I would carry her limp body back home for her nap. I remember searching the internet for some kind of resource for a two-year-old. We watched Muzzy, learning Spanish. We did animal dancing exercise videos on Youtube. We strolled around the neighborhood again and again and again. The same scene, the same trees, the same sidewalk cracks. It was sweet at times, maddening others.

I remember crying in my bed while she watched TV. I remember having panic attacks at night in my husband's arms. I remember often having two drinks on an empty stomach while I prepared dinner. I remember zoning out, smoking spliffs in my small backyard in the evening after she went to bed. I can't recall much else, though countless more hours passed during that time. My parents helped with my daughter sometimes; my brother's girlfriend stepped in for a few hours some Saturdays. But it wasn't enough.

Eventually her daycare opened up again, four months later. She went back to part-time. I started the process all over—feeling the feelings, crying the tears, raging the rage. Slowly my spirit rekindled and my zest for life came back. It was different, though.

Our dreams of close-knit community were bulldozed. The fragile new sprouts of relationships we had created over the few months before the pandemic were stunted. Gathering in groups was no longer acceptable...and though we did it a bit, it was strained, stressful, scary. Everything was different. Everything was harder.

———

I found a new lover over the summer—a beautiful younger woman—who infused my life with joy and sensuality. It was enlivening, invigorating, something exciting in all the drudgery. For a time it gave me a deeper sense of community, of closeness, of connection beyond our two-parent household. We broke up after a few months, but it helped. It even made my relationship with my husband stronger.

———

At the end of summer, our little family bought a house. It was a spot of hope in a year of darkness. It's a small house on a big property. It needed new floors and new paint. It's now fashionably off-white inside with black fixtures and accent walls of deep purple. I'm proud of what we've shaped it into. There are indoor plants everywhere, thriving from my care. There is a large garage at the back of the property that we are going to fix up and use as a gathering space, an event place. It has a lot of potential, and now that the intensity of the pandemic is starting to ease up, we are getting ready to make our dreams of hosting community here a reality.

But last year, when we bought it, things were different. We didn't have a housewarming party. We didn't get to invite people in and celebrate together like we dreamed. We were there, tending a full acre by ourselves. I drank a lot. Too much. I finished bottles of wine by myself, drank through the gin faster than I meant to. It made things feel better, temporarily. In reality, it made everything worse. It put even more distance between me and my husband. It cranked up my anxiety and depression when I wasn't drunk. It helped me suppress the fear and feelings while drinking, but amplified them when I wasn't. I also smoked weed every single day. It made me tired, lazy, exhausted. I still could get things done, but it was only the very bare minimum. I was lonely, tired, hungry for life to have some semblance of normalcy, thirsty to find my soulful spark again, desperate for inspiring connection with other people and time alone.

Eventually we formed a little social pod with another family and a few other friends. They came over some-times, we sat around fires together, had some hot-tub nights. It got a little better. It got a little more hopeful. My bond with my husband got better and worse, better and worse. We made progress, we found hope, we slipped backward, we found more to process. We are still in that dance. We are still together, still strong in our vows and commitment, yet no longer living in the illusion that marriage is easy. We've put polyamory on hold for now to fully focus on healing our love.

We found a different school for our daughter that is a better match. After a few months there part-time, she started full-time again. I started writing again. I started dreaming again. I started feeling my joy return.

This is the short story. This is the overview. The past year was more nuanced, more challenging, more intense than these few paragraphs can tell.

———

It's been over a year now in this surreal pandemic reality. It's been six months since my daughter went back to school full-time. It's been four months since I've been totally sober again. It's been three months since I started a new business.

I'm thriving now in a lot of ways. All that work I did to find myself in motherhood before the pandemic hit really worked. Though it got buried and brushed aside in the depths of lockdown, it didn't die. Once the conditions were ripe, I began to bloom again. It's spring now. The sun is out. The birds are singing and chirping in the trees. I feel a buoyancy in my heart, a joy in my eyes, a bounce in my step. I feel a lusciousness in my hips, a sensual spark, an inner empowerment.

Once I processed the layers of grief, rage, sadness, anxiety, loneliness, and terror the pandemic brought on, once I had more consistent childcare...I found myself again. Another version of myself, again.

Now here I am, a year and a half after I began writing this book. It's finally time to write the ending, this ending, and bring it into the world. I had let go of this project throughout the bulk of the pandemic— too lost, too challenged, too overwhelmed to think about the publishing process. The bulk of this story took place over the course of only six months. Then, it sat on the shelf for a full year, until now.

———

This year has aged me and grown me. I feel like a real adult for the first time. At the ripe age of thirty-four, I truly feel like a woman. I am grounded in my body. I am productive in my creativity. I have built a thriving business based on my love for writing and my passion for guiding people in deep experiences. It's a real, solid business and I am financially successful again for the first time since I became a mom.

My Memoir Coaching business is a miracle, a pinnacle of accomplishment for me. In two weeks I will begin guiding a group of ten women on a ten-month journey to write their own transformational true stories. I built a business out of my deepest creative joy in a way that works with my motherhood lifestyle—one that is grounded in purpose, in service to something greater than me...and it worked. It actually fucking worked.

I searched my soul for months to find what was worth doing, what I could create that actually fits with my limited schedule and allows me to still show up as mom and householder. Something flexible but deep, somewhat easy for me yet intellectually stimulating, something I could do part-time but still make a great income. I hired a business coach and she helped me make it happen. She guided me through the social media marketing, the advertising copy, the enrollment process. Everything. And here we are now, a group of women dedicated to writing the truth, getting ready to dive in and do it together.

The women who have joined my program are incredible. Seven out of ten of them are mothers themselves. They are brave. They are determined. They have something worth saying, worth hearing. They have their own important pieces of the puzzle of liberation and healing to contribute to the global conversation. They are healers, teachers, social workers, mental health advocates, channels, yogis, powerhouses, tender hearts. They are ready to record their true stories and share them with the world, just like me.

I will only be working very part-time, but have brought in more money for the year than I ever have in my life. My husband has started taking on some more domestic duties in order to balance out our arrangement now that I'm working. It's still a process to create a more equitable household. It's still not fair—I have way more of the home load, the emotional labor load, the childcare load, the scheduling and tracking load. But I'm hopeful. I'm hopeful that as I go deeper into this new life of career and wife, author and mother, businesswoman and householder—that we will find our groove.

We are not fully there yet. Sometimes I get over-stressed. Sometimes I get resentful when I'm cleaning the kitchen again and he's on a bike ride. Sometimes I loathe that I have to work only part-time and keep my business small while he gets to scale and soar. Sometimes I get fearful that we will slide right back to the way things used to be, the way things were for much of this book. Especially when unexpected things arise—like my mom is too busy with the restaurant and not able to take care of my kid, or my child gets sick and has to stay home from school—I'm the one that still has to pick up the slack, to drop what's on my plate and pick up the extra one.

There are still kinks to work out. There is still socialization to undo. There are still financial realities that make us have to prioritize his work when the going gets tough. But we are thinking about it, working on it.

We will create a new way: one that fully honors our souls and our needs. One that gives us each time alone, time to recharge, time to play, time for sex and love and friendship, time for nature and for each other. It will probably require more village, more people, more help.

This two-parent model is unsustainable. We have worked with it as best we can, brought in childcare and grandparents and once-in-awhile babysitters. But in the future I see us having more support in a dependable, integrated way. Someone else that can help with the house. Someone who can be a loving presence for our daughter, give us more space so we can actually have lives outside of careers and parenting and not be in this constant grind of way too much work. At least one other person. Ideally a whole community. A real community that cares for each other—beyond capitalism. Beyond individualism. I don't know if it will ever happen, but I pray about it. I wish for it. I dream into it.

After all, it takes a village, as they say. We need more than this mixed-up modern way life has allowed us. It's not healthy for two parents to try to do everything—maintain the house, work fulfilling careers, do all the scheduling, provide the child's emotional needs, drive them to school, pick them up, take them to swimming lessons, make sure there's enough food around, cook all the food, put the kid to bed, wake up with them in the morning and then try to have some kind of romantic relationship even though there is barely any time or energy left for that when everything else is finally done.

Our village right now is my parents, my brother's girlfriend, and my daughter's teacher. They help raise her so I can be a whole and complete human. They help care for her so she can also grow into a well-rounded person with multiple loving influences and a healthy attachment style that is versatile, broad, inclusive. Having support outside our nuclear home makes sense for all of us. It supports my daughter, it enlivens my parents, it gives my brother's girlfriend a chance to bond with a kid and be of service, it helps the school financially, and most of all, it supports me, and us, to be happier and more fulfilled as parents. This is normal. This is natural. This is the healthy order of things.

———

I know we are on the right track because my daughter is thriving. She is continuing to grow in the direction of a well-adjusted, incredibly talented, wonderful human.

My parents watch her two afternoons after school to give me even more space and time to both work and care for myself. In my free time, when I'm done with work and writing, I go on hikes, commune with nature, self-pleasure, relax in the hot tub, tend to my garden. It's a good life right now.

It's fragile, though—anything could happen and change the balance, shift the schedule, throw off the ecosystem. But right now, it feels healthy and sustainable. I have enough time and space to both work and play, build and relax, be myself and tend to others.

The self I am being in this post-pandemic reality is different. My creativity is different. I am not bursting with expression like I was over a year ago, right before this whole ordeal started. I am not skipping through the forest with joy. I am not singing and dancing everywhere. I don't feel a pull towards the performing arts like I did. I'm definitely no longer a comedian, at least not right now. The pandemic and sobriety have changed me. My energy is different. My outlook is different.

My creativity is no longer a hot electric current, sizzling from the inside, sparking all around me. It's a slow, sultry simmer, deep burning embers. It's not a flash of power, splashing color everywhere...it's brown like the earth, green like the trees, held securely within, gently, reliably, consistently moving life forward like a trickling spring that feeds a river. It's less maiden, more mother. It's less mother, more crone. It's wise. It's sustainable. It won't burn out or run out.

My sensuality is reawakening again too, similarly and differently. It is also not in a rush, not flashy, not unbearably alive. It is here, simmering, a vital and necessary part of me.

My friendships are rekindling, growing. Now that it's warm, we will start hosting some outdoor concerts and events in our huge backyard, creating a space for community that honors the complexity of this pandemic era. Ecstatic Dance is back in a large outdoor space, accessible for all. We didn't have that outlet all winter and spring. But now we will go once in a while and charge up our bodies and souls with movement and friendship.

———

Life's not perfect. There are still challenges. There's still stress. There's still anxiety and discontent. I still need space sometimes. I still get overwhelmed and want to run away. But not always. Not often. Not seriously. I'm here to stay. And, when I really need some space, I take a night out at a hotel or go camping. It works out just fine. It gives me the calm and perspective I need to return to my family the next day with gusto and gratitude.

I found a way to prioritize myself and my expression within motherhood, even in a global pandemic, and it's sticking this time. I'm a great mom. My daughter is growing and blossoming into such an incredible human. She is three-and-a-half now. She sings and dances, plays pretend, is smarter than I thought possible, blows us away with her vocabulary and understanding. She is deep, complex, silly, loving, creative, incredibly outgoing. She makes friends everywhere she goes. She composes songs and is the life of the party on a dance floor. She's smart and thoughtful. She hugs and loves, jumps and plays, pushes boundaries and breaks my heart open with her tenderness.

We still have our hardships. It's not always magical. She acts out, frazzles my nerves. She gets in moods of "no" and screams and kicks. It can be frustrating, painful, agonizing. I run out of patience sometimes. I run out of smiles. But for the most part, it's good. It's better. Our relationship is healthy. Our family is healthy. We are all growing and healing together in a never-ending process.

———

For over three years I have been on this path of uncovering my truth, unearthing my pain, undoing eons of women's oppression, and finding myself in this journey of motherhood. I now know that there is no final destination. The journey keeps morphing, changing, going.

I am committed to staying the course, to rebalancing when things get out of whack, to undoing assumed gender roles and finding ways to parent and run a home that actually works for me, for all of us. I am dedicated to taking space and time for myself when I need it so I can be a better mom, a better wife, a better human. So I can be an example of that for my daughter—so she can grow up in a home and a world where women's needs matter, where mothers are allowed to have selves outside of their roles, where the female soul and expression is truly valued. I am adamant about continuing to let go of the definitions of motherhood that I have inherited and creating new ones— for me, for my family, and especially for her—so she can emerge from childhood as a woman with an example of a healthier and happier way to do life.

I am done with the drained and damaged mother archetype. I am over the depleted, harmfully selfless version of womanhood. I will take time and space for myself and not feel guilty. I am determined to live a life I love even within my responsibilities and be so filled up that I naturally give back to the world and people around me. I have everything I need to make this a reality and am gaining more resources every day. Therefore, I know it will be so.

afterword

E diting this work has been an emotional ride. There was so much strife, so much longing, so much hardship recorded on these pages, over this time period. Through reworking these pages I've had to dip back into feeling those things—the frustration, the rage, the sadness, the grief, the resentment. Shaping this work into a book has helped me heal a layer deeper—to feel it, look at it, embody it, let it go.

The biggest emotion I've felt through the editing process, though, is pride. It's "holy shit, I'm actually doing this. I actually did it."

Reading back and seeing how desperately important this writing was to me, how much it was my lifeline, the thing that helped me hold on when I thought I surely would die—is incredible.

Even in all that pain, confusion, struggle—I did it. I kept doing it. I kept going and going and now I am here, editing this book, getting it ready for publication. I kept moving forward despite all the setbacks. I kept doing what made me come alive, even when I felt dead inside. I kept writing, I kept dreaming, I kept living into my truth that I can and will have it all—family and career, home and freedom, husband and lovers, myself and motherhood.

It takes work. It will continue to take work. All of this does not come easy. But still, I persevere.

And the payoff—the moments when I can step back and look at everything I've accomplished, everything I've lived through and survived and grown through, everything I am still becoming—is absolutely worth it.

I am more comfortable in my own skin than ever before. I am more beautiful, too, even with my new wrinkles, gray hairs, and extra padding. I look in the mirror and see someone I admire, someone I trust, someone I love. I see someone of strength, substance, integrity, and more power than I knew I had. I became all those things by forging a path through motherhood that actually works for me. For that, I am incredibly grateful for this journey of being a mom. And...there is so much more. More to learn, more to do, more to be, and more to become. After all, we are only three years in. It has only just begun.

about atmosphere press

Atmosphere Press is an independent, full-service publisher for excellent books in all genres and for all audiences. Learn more about what we do at atmospherepress.com.

We encourage you to check out some of Atmosphere's latest releases, which are available at Amazon.com and via order from your local bookstore:

The Swing: A Muse's Memoir About Keeping the Artist Alive, by Susan Dennis

Possibilities with Parkinson's: A Fresh Look, by Dr. C

Gaining Altitude - Retirement and Beyond, by Rebecca Milliken

Out and Back: Essays on a Family in Motion, by Elizabeth Templeman

Just Be Honest, by Cindy Yates

You Crazy Vegan: Coming Out as a Vegan Intuitive, by Jessica Ang

Detour: Lose Your Way, Find Your Path, by S. Mariah Rose

To B&B or Not to B&B: Deromanticizing the Dream, by Sue Marko

Convergence: The Interconnection of Extraordinary Experiences, by Barbara Mango and Lynn Miller

Sacred Fool, by Nathan Dean Talamantez

My Place in the Spiral, by Rebecca Beardsall

My Eight Dads, by Mark Kirby

Dinner's Ready! Recipes for Working Moms, by Rebecca Cailor

about the author

Flow Belinsky is here to co-create a world where mothers have everything they need to thrive. She lives, works and plays in Bend, Oregon with her husband, daughter and growing community. In her free time, she dances in forests and learns everything she can about regenerative gardening.

If you feel a pull towards telling your true story through memoir, get in touch. Flow passionately guides other women to create their memoirs. She would love to support you to write your way to more wholeness and bring your book to the world.

Learn more here: www.flowbelinsky.com

Made in the USA
Las Vegas, NV
08 April 2023

70366106R00163